Dedicated to the beloved divine (Mother) Sophia, the divine feminine energy of our time. She guides us in self-transformation. She pushes us from the mountainous edge of life experiences. She encourages us to live the fullness of life and walk the middle path as self-aware, divine human beings.

In loving memory of my mother, who, after her transition forty years ago, taught me to walk in the depths of the valley that I may soar from the mountaintop one day.

My mother's mother, Grandmother Sally—your steadfast love, wisdom, compassion, and spiritual teachings fostered my intuition, creativity, and ability to discern the voice of soul and the call of nature. Thank you for feeding me words of wisdom when I was young. It all came back to me when I needed it most.

To my beautiful family: Ray, Ryan, Justin, Jaimie, and Sophia—you teach me every day to surrender to the moment and enjoy life's adventures. My brother Dave—you inspire me with your tenacity and positive attitude. To my dear cousin Maureen—your soulful essence and understanding keep me going in times of challenge. May we continue to grow our love, joy, and wisdom in the years to come. I love you so much!

ACKNOWLEDGMENTS

To all my wisdom teachers on this plane and beyond—you have paved the way for me to stand in the light of soul and shine forth to be of service in the world. I am deeply grateful.

To many special friends and teachers near and far, old and new, on this plane and in the great beyond—I am deeply grateful for your support, encouragement, unconditional love, and blessings: Jill, Kristin, Shiela, Claire, Joni, Mary Ann, Sarah, Jeanne, Linda, Edie, Dana, Ami, Kelly, Peggy, Lynnie, Susan, Lynn, Jodie, Kris, Kim, Alyssa, Atonka, Lydia, Suzanne, Wolfgang, Thupten, Terry, Kunter, Gretchen, Magdalena, Victoria, Cam, Elina, James, Sam, Melissa, Lorraine, and Brenda. To all my friends and loved ones, named and unnamed—to the seamless reality we weave in synthesis of self. I love you!

I'd like to thank the Syinthesis® Sound Healing Community in Glendale, Wisconsin, for your dedication in the evolution of your souls and for participating in my Lotus Heart Sound Journey™ to foster the realization of One-Self. Your presence and enthusiasm in growing our community continues to create a beautiful ripple effect touching all those in its wake—an awakening vibration of peace, love, joy, goodwill, solidarity, and wholeness. I have love and gratitude for you being You!

Alissa Effland, art director extraordinaire, my soul sister— thank you for helping me manifest this dream to share View from the Mountaintop at a higher turn of the sacred spiral. You are brilliant in creative technique and soulfully aligned, birthing the vision from a subtle framework into physical form. You are amazing! I give a deep bow to you.

Evelyn Terranova, your diligent focus and spiritual awareness soulfully ignited within to creatively manifest the cover art. Each step you took was methodical, purposeful, grounded, and divinely light and free. You captured the essence of this work, Evelyn. Thank you!

Linda Neff, dear friend and soulful journeyer, your mindful intention and diligent use of *View from the Mountaintop* as your daily oracle have touched many people around you. This new version has been inspired by you sharing with me the spiritual synchronicities you experienced based on your use of the book as an oracle. Thank you for being the divine spark of light you are.

Catherine Knepper, my editor and friend, I appreciate your ability to flow with the vibration of my intention and maintain integrity in the work while guiding the words to blossom into their full potential. You are a gift. Thank you!

And to Cathryn Denny, the illustrator of the original text, your inner wisdom and intuitive hand created graphics beautifully aligned with the poems. With a full heart, I thank you for heeding the call to work with me in the early '90s. I give a deep bow.

My wish is to awaken the divine in every person I meet in my sound healing journeys, through the poetic verse in *View from the Mountaintop: A Journey into Wholeness*, and through casual invitations to conversation. Imagine standing together in a circle, hand in hand, imbued in the sacred energy of the interconnectedness of life while we envision a more enlightened global consciousness for all.

Upon the mountaintop, we sound forth the clarion call of clarity—that we are One. As we soar unencumbered upon the sacred sound stream, we pave the way for the Sophianic impulse, transforming the self and thus transforming our planet. The hum of the Universe is our lifeblood. We are made of the stars. Saint Francis of Assisi said, "We are the divinity we seek." And when we realize the One-Self, all else is realized; everything just *is*. May the view from the mountaintop be yours.

TABLE OF CONTENTS

FOREWORD

Dear fellow traveler,

As you begin reading the divinely inspired poems composed by Lee Ann Fagan Dzelzkalns in her beautiful *View from the Mountaintop*, you may come to recognize Lee Ann as a heart friend—the friend who genuinely sees you and your heart; the friend listening intently, providing space for silence and reflection; the friend showing up with the exact right words when you need her most.

Working with Lee Ann's poems as part of my morning quiet time practice, I found that her words deeply connect with my own heart. Each poem is crafted with impeccable pacing for the silence and reflection my heart desires. Her words show up in divine right time and right order as either the balm, the tension, or the direction for my heart's own awakening, remembering, and highest knowing.

May you too discover Lee Ann as your heart friend in this magnificent collection of poems that are as simple and as complex as your heart requires. While I enjoy working with the poems as an oracle, you will discover the ways in which Lee Ann's poems best resonate with your beautiful heart. Because, after all, we are each our own best guide, navigating our uniquely divine journeys into wholeness of soul with heart friends at our sides.

With thanks and appreciation for Lee Ann Fagan Dzelzkalns—wise guide, teacher, and heart friend.

Linda Neff
Soul on a journey

AN INVITATION TO JOURNEY WITH ME

It is with joy and gratitude that I welcome you to the second edition of *View from the Mountaintop: A Journey into Wholeness*, celebrating the twenty-fifth anniversary of the book's publication. Whether you are new to *View* or a seasoned reader of contemplative writing, you can journey into the experience, sit quietly with the poem of your choice, or ask a question that is on your heart, pause for a moment, and then turn to a page. The poetic resonance in the poem will reveal a gift to you. There are new daily declarations of empowerment that accompany each poem and serve as a point of focus, a vibrational keynote for you to recite silently or aloud. Additionally, the declarations are sequentially presented in the back of the book as cut-out cards for you to shuffle and select, seeking guidance. The declarations are your companions as you endeavor to experience a daily pilgrimage to further awaken you to You.

Pilgrimage is a sacred rite of passage that begins long before you arrive and lasts long after you return home. It helps connect you with the nature spirits and the stars in the night sky. It helps evoke what you knew when you were young while bringing you into full awareness of who you are and who you have always been from the beginning of time. I trust the energetic vibration of both the book and the declarations will direct you in divine guidance to enlighten your gaze and stabilize your inner walking.

When *View from the Mountaintop* was first published in 1995, I was a busy mom enjoying the adventures and challenges of parenthood. I taught body-mind integration part-time at a university and established my holistic consulting business, all while tending to my personal and spiritual growth and development. I had much inner work to do in healing deep emotional pain from the past, particularly filling the holes in my heart around the loss of my mother. Through therapy, daily meditation, sound alchemy, spending time in nature, and the gentle, loving ministrations of the Divine Mother, I have learned to trust the ebb and flow of life, synthesizing lessons learned through the reconciliation of opposites. I have gained a greater understanding of the power of balance, simplicity, and harmony coupled with a grounded stability in self through embodying a heightened sense of awareness and realization. I have learned to traverse the middle way.

A few years after the book was published, I had an insightful moment that came to me with great clarity. It was like an inner shove that pushed me out of a deep sleep. I was to pay close attention to this inner command blazing in my heart as if written in indelible ink upon the forefront of my mind. It was a powerful declaration, an impression connected to my intuition, my soul, and my Source, the Divine Mother. I could not avoid or dismiss it. The message was carried upon the sacred sound stream, expressing that this book had been written in the energetic design of an oracle. In other words, this book is a divination tool to be opened at random to a verse or passage, a practice known as bibliomancy.

The angelic message continued to grab me in a visceral, whole-body experience. It wouldn't let go until I acknowledged the messenger and the message. I realized then that a higher order of angels had come through while I was writing the book in poetic verse. It was this order, called the Dominion, that was shining the light of truth on me to heed the call and guide people to use the book as an oracle, a divination tool of sacred alchemy. The poetic rhythm and sound pattern in the verse provide a harmony that will resonate in the depths of your soul. As Ted Andrews describes in his book, *Sacred Sounds: Magic and Healing Through Words & Music,* the power of the poet-seer is to "write of secret harmonies so that they can resonate on levels not often recognized. Poetry breathes life into imagined worlds." I felt the touch and guidance of the Great Mother lead me in rekindling my love for writing poetry again.

The essence and presence of the Divine feminine has always guided and supported my every step, but it became more recognizable to me after my mother died in 1980. I had an auspicious, divine direct experience with my mother ten years after her death that led to the creation of this work. I was returning from a business trip where I was facilitating a workshop on treasure mapping at Pepperdine University in Malibu, California. I was flying home, relaxing to music. Then it happened: my entire inner landscape shifted from gentle resting into traversing the inner dimensions, with my mother appearing in full view. I saw myself as an outside observer and simultaneously felt myself standing upon a mountaintop as my mom walked toward me in a flowing, white, gauzy gown.

She seemed to appear as light as air. She approached me and didn't say one word physically; yet she spoke to me psychically. We stood side-by-side on top of the mountain. She lovingly reached for my hand, gesturing for me to follow her lead as she leaned forward, freefalling from the summit. Hand in hand, we fell into the open expansiveness of sky, flying unencumbered and light rather than falling encumbered and heavy.

She then spoke to me. Her lips didn't move; yet the words came forth with clarity and intention. "Honey," she said, "it is time for you to let me go so I may be free and that you may be free." There were no more words. We flew back to the same mountaintop. Our feet touched the surface of the summit as if in slow motion. She departed in a floating fashion into the distance, turned around, and winked at me, as if she were saying, "You've got this." Then she dissolved into nothingness.

I returned to normal consciousness with a tear-drenched face, mindfully sweeping the emotional waters away. I stared at a point of focus in front of me to recount the experience and recapture what my mother said. From this moment, I began to consciously let her go as well as the concept of my attachment to her. I did not want to hold her soul back from evolving or myself from being attached to what was. I realized she is with me every moment through my heart. From this moment, I dove deeper into my journey of self-renewal and wholeness. From that moment, my life opened up into its complete fullness and creative expression, leading me to learn and write about the life lessons I've learned and to share them with others. It is from my experience with Mom that the title of this book is drawn and this book has become a symbolic guide to facilitate the birthing of self into the One-Self.

Since its publication, many individuals have been attracted to the radiant carrier wave of healing vibration in this book. Others are drawn to the message of the verse and the specific titles of the life lessons. Whatever invites you in, what I have come to realize is that the transmission of empowered Grace synthesized through the verse, page by page, is a gentle and generous guide—if you allow yourself to follow your intuition and feel into it. Your higher senses will take over if you give yourself permission to be neutral and stand at the midpoint of opposites. You will learn to balance the extremes and experience you merging with You. You will come to find the still point of your being poised in presence, living in the present moment of awareness.

A veil will be lifted before you so that you may see more clearly and hear more keenly. You will begin to step gently into the full expression of yourself as you are ready. If you don't think you are ready, your soul will prompt you as you listen within. Life lessons, however, unfold before you when your soul invites you to learn from a person, situation, reading, or circumstance to open you up from the inside out. This is the only way we consciously grow, evolve, and expand. We must open the doors within to the heart of our truth. Remember the Little Prince: "It is only with the heart that one can see rightly, what is essential is invisible to the eye." We must be able to feel without a doubt what is the way of the Way, the way of the heart, the way of love. We listen within and heed the call of our wise inner teachers, our souls.

This book is the result of a slow and steady incubation, an organic overture of purpose, preparation, and personal readiness all wrapped up into one fine orchestration. I trust and know the gifts of spiritual alchemy presented between the covers of this book are yours to receive. Receive the resonant frequency of the gifts woven into the rhythm and vibration of the intentional verse, the gifts your soul is placing before you to grow and evolve in the oneness and wholeness of All That Is. Enjoy in joy—yes!

Love and harmony,
Lee Ann Fagan Dzelzkalns

PREFACE

Belief is the key that opens the gateway door.
Truth of the Divine Spark within
expands consciousness to soar.

I was nudged out of bed at 2:00 a.m. by a deep sense of knowing. Inspiration and a flow of words streamed through my consciousness as my hand wrote voraciously to keep up. Shortly after, it dawned on me that I had prayed a week prior for my love of creating poetry to reveal itself again. I wanted so much to write as I did when I was a young girl. This time, however, the verses were filled with clarity and purpose.

For months, I continued to express from my essence words that lovingly guided and directed my life's intention. The entire concept of wholeness, coupled with the symbology of the triangle, kept echoing in my altered state. Each individual poem seemed to place itself in an order of rightness. This natural order then manifested into gateways of self-awareness, self-expansion, and self-realization. It became clearer that the nature of being whole is my understanding of harmonizing and synthesizing the physical, mental, emotional, and spiritual self, which leads to a greater sense of knowledge and wisdom.

This book of poems is an esoteric interpretation of my journey toward wholeness, as the message in each poetic life lesson paves the way for new beginnings. Although our lessons are individual in nature, we can all learn from one another's experience. These thoughts and insights serve as a guide. They explain how conditioned we are and what we need to do to expand our sense of self. These lessons of understanding, forgiving, releasing, accepting, knowing, trusting, and unconditionally loving provide a conduit for the integration of mind, body, and spirit—our essence.

Your essence (that is, your true state of being, the individual connected to the ultimate divine nature of the self, as opposed to existence itself) has always been whole. Yet somehow, you—like so many others—have drifted apart from knowing your goodness and greatness in wholeness. Now is the time to embrace your essence and willingly expand your concept of self.

The head (ego) can keep you very busy in the external world of form (i.e., doing this, doing that, running as fast as you can on the treadmill of life). The dis-ease (as opposed to disease) of encumbered living produces traumatic overtures in your sense of wellbeing. It can keep you far, far away from the inner reality of your true essence. When the ego is fragmented, the physical body is not happy, the mental body is caught in negative cycles, and the emotional body is on the "poor me" path. The ego maintains a grip on the past by replaying old scripts (i.e., thoughts of failure or feelings of inadequacy) and firmly spearheads the emotionalizing of the self. Until you make a choice to break the cycle of fear, anger, resentment, self-doubt, self-rejection, or whatever it is that besets you, you will be caught in its continuous cycle. Know that it is within you to harmonize and synthesize the physical, mental, and emotional selves, which will provide a healthy, balanced, and whole personality. Now is the time to open to a shift in consciousness. The ego does not have to be in control. You can learn to recognize the activity of the heart and intuitively follow its signals.

A gateway symbolizes moving from what was in the past to the truth of what is in the moment. Soar beyond the known into the crispness of new beginnings, and create an opportunity to explore, emerge, and expand. Flow and blend with all aspects of your being emotionally, mentally, physically, and spiritually.

Through contemplation, you will make choices and pass through gateways of understanding that gently and mystically guide you toward wholeness. Your individual path embodies a vibration that guides you from the core of your individuality. And yet, as you venture forward in faith and truth, you will revel in the knowledge that what you have been striving to achieve has always been by nature who you are. You will learn that when you release the need to be someone, you realize that you have always been that someone.

As you become fully conscious of all that you are, you can allow the infinite creative potential to reach the heavens from your depths, for the heavens lie within. As you take this perspective of wholeness, voyage inside to your cellular being, and acknowledge all your goodness, worth, strength, and peace, you will make yourself available to commune with the Essence of all and ignite your inner flame in rightness and truth. (This Essence, with a capital E, is the ultimate divine nature of the Infinite Self, the Oneness of Source, illumined within us.)

This is a journey of life, your personal journey. The poems will guide you along in what may feel like a flowing, synchronous, eternal moment. You may find the words gripping you when you least expect it. You may feel the pages hugging you when you need a hug. You may sense the gentleness of the rhythm and rhyme comforting you as if lulled in a rocking chair. You may experience a rush or release of blocked energy leaving your body. You may willingly receive a gush of love pouring off the page into your heart. You may encounter an overwhelming sense of self-acceptance and unconditional love. You may experience an instantaneous healing. Be open to receive. Let yourself be with the words, verse, and essence of it all.

I know there is great truth in what is presented to you between the covers of this book. The gifts you may receive will be unique and individual to you. I encourage you to remain open and willing to the unlimited possibilities within.

Now, I recommend that prior to reading *View from the Mountaintop: A Journey into Wholeness*, you sit in your quiet center and get comfortable. Then turn to a desired poem or allow your fingers to be guided to the poem that is meant for you in the moment. You may find shuffling the oracle cards (nestled in the back of the book) the perfect tool to use when seeking guidance. Release yourself in the dance of the inner rhythm vibrating amidst the boundless, infinite universal realm of All and take in the view of the mountaintop. Through your own self-exploration and self-discovery, you will experience the essence of being whole.

Love,
Lee Ann

THE SOURCE OF ALL BEING
AND INTERCONNECTEDNESS OF LIFE

How we individually label and call upon the Source of our existence is a private and personal expression. To maintain a sense of universality within this book, I use several names for Source, such as Essence, God, and Truth. I encourage you to replace my terms with what resonates with you.

You may also try to work through the discomfort, trusting in what feels right. Get with someone to share and discuss what is being impressed upon you. You may discover, as I have, that although we practice diverse beliefs, religions, and rituals, the underlying foundation for all is unconditional love. This unconditional love is what we all connect to our individual Source. The words may be different as we pray, but a common ground is shared in our belief in the oneness and interconnectedness of life.

We are already one. But we imagine that we are not, and what we have to recover is our original unity. What we have to be is what we are.
—Thomas Merton (Christianity)

God is like a mirror. The mirror never changes but everyone who looks at it sees a different face.
—Midrash Tanhama (Judaism)

All life is one. The world is one home. All are members of one human family. All creation is an organic whole. No man is independent of this whole. Man makes himself miserable by separating himself from others. Separation is death. Unity is eternal life.
—Sivananda (Hinduism)

Do you think that God is only in your heart? You should be able to recognize Him in every garden, in every forest, in every house, and in every person.
—Shams of Tabriz (Sufism/Islam)

One perfect nature pervades and circulates within all natures. One all-inclusive Reality contains and embraces all realities. One moon is reflected in every expanse of water. Every reflected moon is one moon. The essence of all Buddhas is in my being. My essence is in their being.
—Zen Master Yung-Chia Ta-Shih (Buddhism)

There is only one God, all the 'gods' are but His ministering angels who are His manifestations.
—Omoto Kyo, Michi-no-Shiori (Shinto)

Every object in the world has a spirit and that spirit is Wakan. Thus the spirits of the trees or things of that kind, while not like the spirit of man, are also Wakan. Wakan comes from the wakan beings. They are never born and never die. They can do many things that mankind cannot do. Mankind can pray to the wakan beings for help. The word Wakan Tanka means all of the wakan beings because they are all as if One.
—Sword, a Native American Dakota (Native American)

Mysteriously existing before heaven and earth. Silent and empty. An unchanging oneness. An ever-changing presence. The Mother of all Life. It is impossible to really give it a name, but I call it Dao. Without wishing to define it, it could be called The Whole.
—Lao Zi, *Dao De Jing* (Daoism)

There can be no doubt that whatever the peoples of the world, of whatever race or religion, they derive their inspiration from one heavenly Source, and are the subjects of one God.
—Gleanings from the Writings of Baha'uillah (Bahai)

Thank you for your anticipated openness and willingness to lovingly read these words from your heart with your soul.

DAILY PRAYERS AND INVOCATIONS

These prayers and invocations are an offering of love. They are yours to receive and embrace. Use them in conjunction with the book, or offer them up on their own. You may say them in directed consciousness, clearly visualizing the process, or simply be with the essence of your intention. Allow yourself space to get centered (settle your entire being) and be with the verse and your inner guidance. I recommend you practice the daily "Heart of the Equal-Armed Cross" invocation to create a unified field with all of us guided in this soulful inner work.

HEART OF THE EQUAL-ARMED CROSS

Focus in your heart center. See and feel, sense and know your radiant point of light in the center of your chest. Imagine a radiant line of light reaching down to the heart of earth and another line of light reaching up to the heart of heaven, connected vertically above and below. There are imaginary arms of light that reach out right and left from your heart center to all of humanity, sharing your essence in the world. These lines of radiant light from your heart center create an equal-armed cross above, below, within, and without. This powerful symbol represents fairness, justice, equality, balance, harmony, and right relationship. We are the equal-armed cross, carrying the significance of this energy through our heart centers into our daily lives. It touches all those in its wake through the vibration of the positive ripple effect.

Between the heights and the depths, between the within and the without, we are balanced and centered, aligned and harmonic. We are one with All That Is. Imagine we are standing together hand in hand, heart to heart, mind to mind, and soul to soul, sharing peace, love, goodwill, and solidarity for all humanity. May we envision a more enlightened global consciousness for all the world. Invoke the equal-armed cross during the course of your day to hold true to the symbolism, centering in your heart and feeling the emanation of your lines of light being your equal-armed cross, being the love, being the light, being all that you are, simple and true, being you.

May we give thanks for our shared consciousness and for all that is and so it is and help us all to do our parts.
Amen. Amin. Hum. Om. Shanti. Aho. Yes!

GROUP INVOCATION ON WHOLENESS

As we lovingly invoke the hierarchy of Divine wisdom, we humbly give thanks for this shared consciousness.

May we always be aware as we awaken to our realization, our connectedness to Source and the kingdom within.

May our minds be open to the Divine illumination of Truth.

May our hearts reveal their essence of unconditional love.

May our bodies be healthy, harmonious, disciplined homes for our souls.

May our souls be infused with integrated joyful personalities.

May our intuitive eyes clearly see our lives' purpose.

May our words communicate with clarity and compassion.

May our eyes bless all that we behold.

May our energies be in atonement with infinite Source/ Essence/God.

May the nature of wholeness and unconditional love be awakened in the heart and soul of our planet.

We lovingly allow these qualities to stream forth to nourish and illumine universal consciousness in humankind.

Amen. Amin. Hum. Om. Shanti. Aho. Yes!

THE ESSENCE AND PRESENCE OF DIVINE SOPHIA

We lovingly invoke your Essence and Presence, Divine Sophia, known to many as White Buffalo Calf Woman in the Native American tradition, Wisdom Sophia in Judaism, Khalq in Sufism, Shaki Kali Devi in Hinduism, Shekinah in the Kabbalah, Quan Yin in Buddhism, Tara in Tibetan Buddhism, Wu Ji in Taoism, Isis in Egyptian, and Wisdom in Greek. We are the weavers of synthesis, blending any/all sense of duality into the harmonic still point of our non-dual nature, unity consciousness.

WE GIVE THANKS TO YOU, DIVINE MOTHER

Oh, Divine Mother of life,
through your pulse, we resonate in divine flow,
a truth-filled rhythm of synthesis.

Oh, Divine Mother of love and wisdom,
we give thanks our hands are guided to reach
and help hearts and souls of all humankind.

Oh, blessed Mother of light,
as we nourish and strengthen our containers of self,
may we come into full expression of One-Self
to live the holy grail with you.

It is through the mirror reflection
we see your sustaining beauty, our truth.
We give thanks between the heights and the depths,
between the within and the without.
We are centered and balanced,
aligned and harmonic with you.

We give thanks,
oh wise Mother of creative power,
as we walk together in love.
We feed our souls, fill our hearts, clear our minds,
ground our bodies, and enlighten our gazes
in the awakening frequency of your Sophianic impulse.
Divine love streams forth into our united beings
now and forevermore.

Amen. Amin. Hum. Om. Shanti. Aho. Yes!

PRAYER OF SERVICE

I am flowing love, light, and presence
as I blend with the highest of Essence.
I am open and available in this day
to God's grace and unfolding way.

A NIGHTTIME WISH

As I wish upon this star,
my intention travels, jettisoning far.
Lifting to the Essence known,
the realm of guidance I am shown.

PRAYER OF PROTECTION

I pray for protection in the name of universal
peace and love
and in the light of the omniscient Oneness
within and above.
This power is stronger than any power
known in heaven and earth,
gently guiding my hand from the beginning
of time, any birth.

I pray for the protection of my aura
sealed in a cone of light,
laced in the brilliance of gold and white,
a mirror reflection so bright.
Anything of the false nature bounces off
this suit with care,
sending back to the source rightness
from the Essence we share.

I thank you, universal Essence/God,
for your loving protection this day
as I continue to serve from my heart,
the love, the light, and the Way.

I AM THANKFUL

I am thankful for the presence of Spirit
unconditionally guiding my hand.
I am thankful for the presence of Spirit
as I feel my heart lovingly expand.

I am thankful for the presence of Spirit
filling my breath with strength.
I am thankful for the presence of Spirit,
patience growing in length.

I am thankful for the presence of Spirit
expressing truth through me.
I am thankful that I have awakened
to reclaim my essence "to be."

I am thankful for the presence of Spirit
enlightening my vision to see.
I am thankful for the presence of Spirit
illuminating my soul through Thee.

I am thankful for the abundance
that is truly mine this day.
I am thankful for the Essence of all;
it is the way of the Way.

Journey of the Self
Toward the Self

A JOURNEY INTO WHOLENESS

You are reading this book for a higher reason than you may consciously know. As you develop your awareness and knowledge about your entire sense of being, you will understand more and more. Your thirst will become voracious as you seek and find answers to questions, solutions to problems, and truths revealed. It's all about acknowledging your higher self, your intuitive self, the will of your soul. (We're really just one great pool of energetic souls waiting to serve the world.) When we open to our essence, the Essence of All That Is can then filter its great love through us so we may serve in all areas of our lives, from play to work. In this service, we discover the sweet scent of life filled with unconditional love and wisdom of the ages.

The poetic words within may gently guide you through the veils of illusion that challenge your physical, mental, and emotional wellbeing. You may break through the obstacles and patterns of conditioned programming such as the need to always be in control, the inability to receive gifts or compliments from others, the refusal to nurture yourself while caring for others, the feelings of inadequacy or not being good enough, the fear of failure, the inability to trust, the inability to share, the need to guard the heart from the pain of the past, and so forth. Conscious awareness will expand your vision to see and acknowledge the fear of the past. Once you recognize the patterns and have the willingness to break them, you are on your way to embracing all your goodness in God-ness.

The spirit of your creative essence will reveal itself as you open to your true nature. Just as (in the story of Capricorn) the goat climbs the mountain and transcends its egoic self into the nature of the unicorn, its true self, you too can emerge into the wholeness of your soul. The separate parts will no longer exist. As you begin the climb to the mountaintop, you move toward balance and unification of the ego/head and the essence/heart. As Cynthia Bourgeault shares in her book *The Meaning of Mary Magdalene,* we gradually begin to transcend our egoic operating systems, learning life lessons while uncovering our higher operating systems, the wisdom of heart.

I have categorized three gateways to assist you in moving along the pathway to reach the mountaintop. Remember, these gateways are mere symbols to your own personal growth and spiritual expansion. It is up to you to reach inside, dig deep, and seek the truth within. It is here where oneness resides. It is here you will come to embrace that you are that which you seek. Saint Francis of Assisi said, "You are the divinity you seek." When you rest in the knowledge that there is nothing to seek because *you are it,* then your inner landscape transforms into a balanced, aligned, and harmonic self. The skills of relaxation, meditation, and contemplation can greatly assist you in this self-discovery and expression. For this purpose, a guided meditation is presented at the back of the book.

Gateway I guides you into the process of purging, releasing, and renewing. This process will repeat itself again, only at a higher turn of the spiral. This means you are growing and evolving soulfully, elevating in consciousness. Surprisingly, you will discover how wonderful it is to completely get in touch with the anxiety and fear that have been embedded in the depths of your cellular memory. Self-exploration will open you to the known in the unknown as you trust in that knowing. This gateway leads through the *deconditioning* of the self. Here, you experience a release of the conditioned habits into a creative consciousness of goodness and unconditional love steeped in a higher sense of awareness. This is a continual process of change and growth. The rendition of this cycle is a psychospiritual rhythm set by your willingness to evolve in your heart, mind, and soul.

Recognize that the cycle will repeat itself when it serves your highest good to advance up the mountain.

Gateway II begins reconditioning the self in a gentle shift of understanding. A positive perspective replaces what was once a negative downward spiral. Here, your conditioned self learns how to break barriers and decondition from old ways to create a new threshold of living. Your *reconditioned* self will embrace the straight and narrow path and seek answers to all questions and contemplative moments. Seek, and you shall find. If you don't ask, how will you ever know? If you don't knock on the door, how can it ever be opened? You will begin to experience your entire sense of being and create adjustments to come into balance, harmony, and synthesis of self.

Gateway III illumines the *unconditioned* self. Think about the possibilities of the unconditioned self. You are free to be all that you are within the realm of all unlimited possibilities, free to be your essence connected to the Essence of All That Is. Yes—to be! You begin to experience the embrace of the oneness in your heart, mind, body, and soul. The light of your soul shines its purpose, connecting within your heart. Here, you approach the top of the mountain and literally feel the emergence of the soul infusing with the body, mind, and emotions. This is where life is lived fully. This is where life is lived wholly. This is the essence of being whole.

As you read this book, imagine yourself somewhere on the mountain trail. Lovingly flow with this image, and trust in the process. In this image, allow yourself to be free of judgment as you page through this book. Read the verses, and then ponder over them. What do they mean to you? Contemplate. Just be with them, and sit in silence. Allow your inner guidance, your higher self and soul, to provide the space to learn spiritual discernment and loving detachment. Just be in the eternal present moment. Fully embody the interconnectedness of life as you express your connection to All That Is.

Gateway 1

Decondition the Self

RELEASE TO SEE

The forest will answer you in the way you call to it.
—Finnish Proverb

To decondition the self is to release yourself from the confines of past judgment and emotional attachment. Awareness and clearing of subconscious cultural and societal programming take place. The judgments of personal perceptions and interpretations lose their influence as you begin to express what is in true affirmation in your life. As you consciously decondition, you can reject the error of false thought, negative thinking, or any idea of lack in your life. Instead, you will own right thinking and the power of knowing your own heart. Through this, you create the ability to discover all that you truly are.

Insights and illuminations will present themselves to you as you awaken your conscious awareness. Effort and commitment to break cycles, move through conditioned patterns, release association of thought, and empty out is a ritual in self-awareness and renewal. Your personal mantra may go from "I know I can; I know I can" to "I am all that I am; I am all that I Am." The leading words, "I am," are how master Jesus declared, affirmed, and brought forth manifestation. "I am" represents being pure, unconditioned consciousness.

Moving through a gateway may be painful at times, but it is part of the learning. Your body will let you know if you haven't dealt with an issue or problem. The emotion will embed further into your cellular memory, building a solid, thick wall of protection. If you notice tightness in your solar plexus, reflect on the immediate situation that stimulated your physiology. The lessons may become clearer. A guarded heart is a major battle to overcome. You may discover your own shielded heart when you begin taking responsibility for your feelings and enforcing self-awareness strategies. When you recognize your patterns of behavior, you can begin to release and break them. As you become aware and accepting of what is, you can then move on to the next unfolding level of self-expansion.

Awaiting you on the other side of the gate is the breath of new beginnings and insights. The duality of my lessons has taught me that peace and happiness can be born from the wisdom in disharmony and sadness. As I become more in touch with my true sense of self, as each layer of conditional, emotional release reveals itself, I am clearer and freer. When I was learning about detachment (which I continue to learn about), I came to realize my attachment to certain things and certain people. I found myself agonizing over how to get to that neutral space in between attachment and detachment. I also found that the power of letting go and trusting in the Essence of All That Is accelerated my process of growth and expansion. I trusted. I cultivated spiritual self-reliance by learning to listen and feel from my heart. When I embraced both ends of the spectrum, dual in nature, (attachment and detachment), I found peace in the neutral space between the two.

To lovingly claim truth in your life, begin with owning your flaws and strengths. Balance of your physical, mental, and emotional self is the first step toward synthesis of the whole self in soul and personality. The journey up the mountain is a climb. With each step, however, we grow closer to our peace of mind, wisdom of the heart, health of the body, and knowledge of the Absolute. With each breath, we renew ourselves into a realm of continual expansion and eternal knowingness—knowledge that we are more than matter in this external world of form; we are spirit manifesting as divine matter.

DECONDITION THE SELF FROM

- the world of glamour
- the seduction of the world in crisis and chaos
- perception of the ego's false importance
- separation consciousness and the sense of duality
- gripping emotions of fear, anger, and loneliness
- self-imposed limits
- debilitating beliefs based on false past perceptions

self-awareness

Time to Fly

Wings spread open;
it's time to fly.
Others will stop you—
or at least, they will try.

Listen to your heart;
the answers are there.
Begin at the start:
love unconditionally; always be fair.

It is in the moment,
as you will see,
that people will either hear you,
be awakened, or flee.

Be true to yourself
in all that you do.
The Essence is Divine.
Now it is time to be you!

———————

DAILY DECLARATION OF EMPOWERMENT
TIME TO FLY

IN THE LIGHT OF MY SOUL, I DECLARE:

I trust in all that I am, in all that I Am.

Lessons

You can go through life without a clue
of what it's all about
or take the time to go within,
unfolding a purposeful route.
Your mission on earth is unique
and special to only you;
it's about learning lessons,
inner strength, and being true.

Others may tell you what to do
as you journey down your path.
Be open in your thought;
release insecurities or feelings of wrath.
Know that you have all the power
within to do great things.
The answers lie at your center:
dig deep; see what it brings.

How do you listen to
what life's lessons really teach?
Wait for unfoldment;
this will challenge you to reach.
Then the impression will come
about what you are to learn.
You will open your awareness
to tackle every turn.

The same lessons come back
time again if you do not act.
This is more than observation;
this is a universal fact.
When you get caught up
in a pattern that won't let go,
recognize what is happening,
then move through it slow.

Realize that life is an educational tool
striving to instruct.
The vision of what we create
for ourselves isn't fate or luck.
What we do with the instruction
and how we learn from it
is the difference between flowing
in life and wanting to quit.

Life's lessons come in all disguises
as you discover within
to further your advancement here,
stretching yourself to win.
It's not about winning a race
or being better than another;
it is inner love, integrity,
and loving your sisters and brothers.

Know the choice is truly yours;
the impression is in your heart.
You decide to learn or not;
there is no trial to finish or start.
Your journey is an accumulation
of everything up until now.
Respect yourself where you are
on your path and lovingly allow.

DAILY DECLARATION OF EMPOWERMENT
LESSONS

IN THE LIGHT OF MY SOUL, I DECLARE:

I open to receive my life lessons
and accept the gift in their revealing.

Acceptance

When you enter into this world, you are filled
with limitless potential.
You have not had much time to be cautioned
about the influential.
But this limitless potential is with you
for all your existence.
You just need to recognize your goodness
with love and persistence.

The fact remains so clear to embrace
all that you are.
Accept yourself for the Essence in you;
let go of contracted scars.
Limiting scars are mental thoughts
produced only by you.
Acknowledge what they are—release them;
say they are through!

Try not to give them power, otherwise
they will grow and grow.
Do you know what I mean?
Have you ever made yourself feel low?
The choice is yours to peer deep
within your heart.
Realize you are a wonderful being,
every inner and outer part.

To accept yourself unconditionally means
there are no limitations
to value yourself as a worthy human being,
an incredible creation.
It really doesn't matter what
other people think.
It is up to you what counts—
this is truly the missing link.

When you believe in yourself and the truth
of your being,
you will open your inner eyes to illumination,
clarity in seeing.
Trust as you go within yourself; flow with
unfoldment of grace.
This is your Essence, your spiritual source—
it will bring light to your face.

As you learn the acceptance of self,
you will live from the inside out.
This will make a difference in daily living
you will see without a doubt.
If you want to change how you view yourself
strictly on the outside,
think about your inner dialog
at the center of which you abide.

You are filled with inner integrity;
honor yourself through and through.
Make the day special, affirm your goodness,
embrace all that is new.
It is in your personal transformation
that growth continues to soar
as you accept the goodness of Grace
bestowed upon you forevermore.

———————

DAILY DECLARATION OF EMPOWERMENT
ACCEPTANCE

IN THE LIGHT OF MY SOUL, I DECLARE:

I love and accept myself unconditionally
as I open my heart to my truth of being.

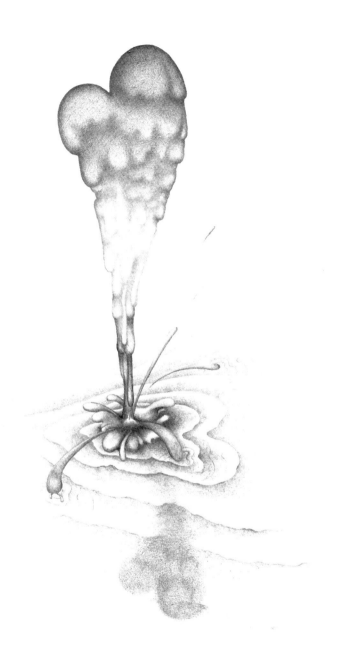

Echo of Love

The vibrational echo of love courses through
all of me,
tracing elements of tranquil living,
pent-up discomfort set free.

Love lingers longingly through my essence,
my savoring soul;
it awakens a yearning and a thirst
to release past perceptions and roles.

For the message of love is overwhelmingly pure
as it reflects the field of Grace,
lifting and clarifying the mystical presence of
white light enveloping Truth's face.

So I clear my thoughts of what it may be
to embrace the moment's perfection of loving
lightly all of Thee.

To dismiss the definition of how others relate
to love
but to feel, taste, and recognize my heart's
echo from the heavens above.

For the dimension of love is beyond all words,
expressed in a humble surround—
a knowingness so deeply imbued, to be lived
and shared, a gift oh so profound:
the echo of love.

DAILY DECLARATION OF EMPOWERMENT
ECHO OF LOVE

IN THE LIGHT OF MY SOUL, I DECLARE:

I am flowing in the stream of divine love.
I share this positive ripple effect with all those in its wake.

Letting Go

Your beingness is light and free,
no matter where you are.
Teach others now about how to be;
they will awaken and reach far.

As you surrender and lift up high
to a knowingness that is real,
stretch yourself to the majestic sky
as feet nestle in the earth to feel.

Rather than question your sense of direction
or why it is up to you,
let yourself make the natural selection;
truly let go, and lovingly do.

———————

DAILY DECLARATION OF EMPOWERMENT
LETTING GO

IN THE LIGHT OF MY SOUL, I DECLARE:

I practice self-emptying. I let go of
inner gripping (attachments).
I create space for love in my life now.

Be Still

The moment of stillness is overwhelming
as you embrace inner peace.
It takes you to a different dimension
very sovereign, provoking release.
To get quiet and go within yourself, to listen
in this meditative state,
is about expanding your awareness, walking
through the spiritual gate.

As you become still in meditation,
you will free your mind of thought.
You will detach from all impressions
and associations you were taught.
Go ahead and discover
the sense of being still;
it is about self-exploration,
choice, and free will.

Stillness evokes an inner thirst
to explore deep beyond,
the connectedness to which
we all tightly form a bond.
Learning to relax, to quiet the mind
and become still,
is a disciplined venture
for the yearning to be filled.

Be filled with the splendor
of the grandness deep inside.
Only you can find it within yourself;
it doesn't try to hide.
Feel the sense of silence draw you
to the center of who you are.
Your conscious awareness expands—
feel yourself moving far.

Let yourself be with this moment;
there are no limits at all.
It is your perception of what it is that
colors or breaks your fall.
Quiet yourself now, be silent,
journey inside far beyond.
Expand the illumination of your light,
your radiance so fond.

Stillness is in the moment,
connecting universal ties—
when you sense discernment, release
yourself; joyfully cry.
It is in the inner knowing
that we are spiritually alive,
celebrating the expansiveness within
as we continue to thrive.

Stillness. Quiet. Within. You are home.

————————

DAILY DECLARATION OF EMPOWERMENT
BE STILL

IN THE LIGHT OF MY SOUL, I DECLARE:

I am radiantly alive in the stillness of my quiet center.
I am pure spaciousness.

Detachment

Does the body know the difference
from reality and not?
Is it encoded in the cells, generating a
stronghold of the lot?
Can it hold the pain and discouragement,
the grief and fear,
resulting in an unconscious accumulation
of sometimes years?

We don't even realize the effect
our lives' woes create
when we manifest illness trying
to make the crooked straight.
Sometimes it is not a conscious act,
although it may seem.
Could we possibly make ourselves sick?
Maybe it's only a dream.

The different areas of the body—muscles
and organs—truly know
that it is time to detach from guilt
and allow love to grow.
What do we do about this powerful connection
of body and mind?
Understand the delicate nature
of attachment and the kind.

Holding on to resentment, anger, fear,
and unconscious stuff
drives a deeper wedge in time
until consciousness says, "Enough!"
Take the time to recognize your feelings;
deal with them now.
It is in the present moment
when you feel empowered—pow!

Function from the core of your being,
the essence of inner truth.
You will begin to release the pain regardless
of pudding or proof.
As you release the control of emotions
that you gave power to,
beyond, you will find a new horizon
for life to travel through.

Detach from the grip of issues
and fears, forgive, and move on.
Release the attachments
of which you have become so fond.
The material possessions
and relationships just the same
can be detached through the love
of the conscious choice game.

You will find that detachment brings freedom,
unity, and space.
It encourages a sense of enlightenment
illumined only by Grace.
Trust your inner guidance
as you willingly detach and let go.
Be all that you are as you soar
in the realization that you *do know*.

———————

IN THE LIGHT OF MY SOUL, I DECLARE:

I am mindfully detaching from what was
that I may open my heart
upon the middle way of nonattachment.

Conditioned Thoughts

Open up your vision to new beginnings now.
See how conditioned thoughts restrict and not allow.
They keep you locked up in your self-imposed chains,
as you struggle desperately to make personal gains.

These conditioned beliefs have been a part of your being.
Take the time to learn from them, eyes open wide for seeing.
Face them, and embrace the fact that they exist in you;
then have the willingness to erase them to create the new.

Conditioned thoughts may perpetuate insecurities and lack.
The control itself is conditioned, unaware of its tact.
Not feeling good enough is conditioning from the past.
Acknowledge these thoughts so they do not have to last.

While the ego nature is most resistant to change,
it is your spiritual unfoldment that compels you to arrange.
As you break up the old patterns conditioned within,
your spiritual-ness will emerge to humbly win.

To win the essence that has always been a part of you,
embrace the exhilaration of feeling whole and truly new.
Experience enlightenment deep within your core.
Step into your inner space; experience peace forevermore.

DAILY DECLARATION OF EMPOWERMENT
CONDITIONED THOUGHTS

IN THE LIGHT OF MY SOUL, I DECLARE:

I allow my rigid held beliefs to melt
into a clarity of what is to be.
I am creating opportunity for the new.

Synchronicity

The rightness of this moment
falls into the lap of time,
not knowing where it's going,
just trusting in the rhyme.

The synchronicity avails itself
of the illusions to be,
detaching self of limitations
to ethereal expansion so free.

Why would we believe that chance
is a guiding light and force
eliminating the moment's trust,
a divinely assisted course?

The rightness delivered is of perfection
as we make our own choice
to follow the loving stillness within
as we trust this inner voice.

The spontaneous presents itself
in myriad ways for us to see
that our spiritual essence will open the door,
free of any key.

We own the knowledge, our birthright,
to be all that we are,
honoring synchronicity,
trusting, reaching far.

Dance in the gentle breeze,
lifting as light as a kite.
Soar in the liberated expression
of the eagle in flight.

It is in the serene knowingness
that inner guidance impresses the heart,
as the synchronous dance of reality
blends wholeness in all its parts.

———————

DAILY DECLARATION OF EMPOWERMENT
SYNCHRONICITY

IN THE LIGHT OF MY SOUL, I DECLARE:

I trust in the unfolding synchronicity of life lessons,
as they are based in the
universal wisdom of Divine right time and order.

The Self

Light of the heavens streams through the clouds,
tenderly touching the earth,
reflecting the waters, drenching the soul,
gracing the self of its worth.
The union of the self converges in synchronicity
for its Essence to be
an age-old dance of the spirit,
the mind extolling jubilant harmony.

The ego self angers at the tarnishing of
its name
while the Essence self remains oh so humble
just the same.
As the elemental self accepts the myriad
of emotions expressed,
it is difficult for the ego to admit,
see truth, and confess.

The elemental self is the basic
intuitive nature within.
The ego self is the personality
in conflict, always trying to win.
The Essence self is the higher order
within, peacefully flying free,
releasing the bondage of separate selves,
creating wholeness in Thee.

So the whole self is more than
just a part of parts to see;
it is the Divine Essence awakening
you to see the real me.

―――――――

IN THE LIGHT OF MY SOUL, I DECLARE:

I am more than a part of parts to see.
I am whole within the Whole, sharing
the full expression of me.

Mirror Reflection

It is in the mirror reflection
that I gain perspective to see
that what I view in you
is what exists in me.

So funny—this universal law
teaches us to learn
that life's lessons clarify
with each and every turn.

As we make the choice
to journey toward the whole,
we reflect off one another
as we justify each and every toll.

What a blessing it is to see
in you the real me.
This is how we awaken ourselves
to release, to expand, to be free.

A tenacious rendition of duality
exists in the guarded fear,
as we attach to our thoughts
through our shielded tears.

Sharing from the heart of compassion
the love of our souls,
revealing the essence of our truth
to gain knowledge, detaching past roles.

So clear the virtue of the self
bounces from this being,
presenting life's lessons, enlightening the
self, transforming inner seeing.

———————

DAILY DECLARATION OF EMPOWERMENT
MIRROR REFLECTION

IN THE LIGHT OF MY SOUL, I DECLARE:

I am choosing to see in you the real me.
This is how I awaken myself to release,
to expand, to be free.

Purpose

Every moment in life is purpose-filled
as we let go and trust in the All,
directing thought in peaceful willingness,
subconsciously guiding the fall.

To lift oneself up is in the notion
of knowing it's not wrong or right—
to experience freedom in space and motion,
moving unencumbered without a fight.

It is a gentle echoed knowingness
with which we choose to act,
to live a life in stateful bliss,
creating purpose regardless of fact.

A fact is in the outer reality
in which we merely exist.
It is in our inner existence
of how we truly subsist.

Yes, our lives' lessons are real,
as we awaken to the intention.
We mindfully choose to listen and feel
our lives' purpose and true direction.

DAILY DECLARATION OF EMPOWERMENT
PURPOSE

IN THE LIGHT OF MY SOUL, I DECLARE:

I listen with inner ears. I see with inner eyes.
My life lessons teach soul's purpose, no matter the disguise.

Gateway 2

Recondition the Self

RENEW TO THEE

When we surrender to our essence,
which is connected to the whole universe,
we resonate with the whole and
pull to us all that is needed.
—Gloria D. Karpinski, *Where Two Worlds Touch*

To recondition the self, embrace the reality of what is and the illusion of what isn't. To think Truth every day is to know reality in our true Essence. Truth is a silent principle. You can learn to silence the noises and mind chatter (illusion) and listen to the silent law that speaks from the True Self within (reality). What you are doing is training the intellect to the passageway of understanding. After you begin to embrace the Essence of all that you are in wholeness, truth and knowledge come forth.

To recondition the self is to recognize and remove layers of illusion in character. You then can begin to release the character of false thinking that causes the dis-ease of humankind. What is held in thought, in the heart, in prayer, and in faith will manifest. As you acknowledge the positive perspective of living a life of simplicity, happiness, and love, so will it be. Shifting my consciousness to right thinking has given me a light, free, positive formula for daily living.

Reconditioning the self is a commitment to seeking the essence of the soul. Preparatory stages toward the unconditioned self are initiated to clear oneself of impurities and balance the mind and body. To recondition oneself is to hold firm to truth, love unconditionally, and demonstrate equality.

As you climb the mountain and ponder your ascension, you will recondition the old cycles and patterns. A newness grows through an emptying out—a replenishing of clarity and clear intention. To continue your journey up the mountain, your inner sights will continue to awaken a balance in your mental, emotional, and physical bodies. You can't help but to achieve an equilibrium of self as you attend to the self and become aware of what is and what isn't. You know. You just know when you listen with inner ears and feel from your heart center. When you begin living life from this vantage point, you will never turn back. The climb up the mountain may appear steep. Yet, in turn, it is a mere twinkling of God's eyes guiding you home.

self-expansion

RECONDITION THE SELF TO

- embrace the process of healing and self-transformation
- free the mind of rigid held beliefs
- calm the emotional body of attachments
- relax, nourish, and nurture the physical body
- ignite your inner flame
- rekindle the sense of wholeness within
- create a fulfilling, positive reality; believe in yourself
- live a purposeful, conscious, giving, loving, caring life
- seek and discover your goodness, beauty, and truth

Reality or Illusion?

Look in the distance, and what do you see?
A merging of the heavens and earth in reality.
But when you reach this point far off,
once a goal-oriented view becomes an illusion aloft.

So how do illusion and reality really compare?
Is it like a mind free of thought, not being aware?
Or is it releasing the contrived world of form,
like when you blend a hot and cold, the end result warm?

Is our reality keenly objective in all that we see?
Or do we narrow our focus to passively agree?
To broaden our perspective defies the social norm
that the mental image of thought is illusion in form.

Don't take this notion seriously, as you will come to find
that everything is an illusion; it will boggle your mind.
Although the world of form seems solid, please guess again.
It's all made up of waves and particles—why, what, and when.

It is the power we give to things, creating a grandiose scheme.
Just try to release association of thoughts as you drift in dream.
Keep yourself uplifted in consciousness in the neutral space.
Whether reality or illusion, it's about living in love and grace.

———————

DAILY DECLARATION OF EMPOWERMENT
REALITY OR ILLUSION?

IN THE LIGHT OF MY SOUL, I DECLARE:

I sit at the midpoint of opposites,
an uplifted, neutral space.
Whether reality or illusion,
I live a life of love and empowered Grace.

Objective Reality

What is this objective reality all about?
Can it really encourage harmony without a doubt?
Does it expand your inner awareness beyond,
where edges of your consciousness unify and bond?

It is in the realm of simplicity that we begin to see
that our objective reality is all possibilities to be.
Realize that life is more than embracing black and white:
it is the space of choice between the
difference of left and right.

The space between opposites gives us room to grow;
it creates an open awareness of possibilities to know.
Our objective reality permits us to expand from within,
learning lessons not from failure or expectation to win.

It is the gentle reminder that possibility does exist
to look at every situation with choices you can enlist.
It is not in the either/or thinking that you need to adhere—
rather, the lighthearted acknowledgment
of releasing the fear.

Fear embeds the cellular level, resisting the seed of change,
hanging, clinging, grasping tightly to
familiar cycles arranged.
Our emotions can paralyze us, inhibiting our ability to grow.
Living from objective reality creates
opportunity to experience flow.

Close your eyes, and envision a cube
on the screen of your mind.
What are you looking for, and exactly what do you find?
Do you see more than one side of this dimensional form,
or are you stuck in a pattern, like fear erupting from a storm?

It is your objective reality that allows you the choice to see.
There are many sides to this cube;
the possibilities are up to thee.
Learn to create balance, harmony, and a free-spirited vision,
embracing the reality that life is possibility
and indeterminant decision.

DAILY DECLARATION OF EMPOWERMENT
OBJECTIVE REALITY

IN THE LIGHT OF MY SOUL, I DECLARE:

I am balanced and harmonic with a free-spirited vision.
I embrace the reality that life is unlimited possibility.

Truth

Trust in the now;
it is the point to be.
You must let go and allow
for all of you to see.

It is not about what was
or what is going to be.
It is the present because
you are you, a part of me.

Forget about what others say
or how they look at you.
Be in your truth each day;
embrace the presence as new.

Feel the gentle whisper
of guidance within your heart.
It is a sense of deep reliance
that is close rather than apart.

The truth is hidden within your soul,
as you have come to know
that life's journey is not a goal
but the unfolding self to grow.

————————

DAILY DECLARATION OF EMPOWERMENT
TRUTH

IN THE LIGHT OF MY SOUL, I DECLARE:

The truth is hidden in my soul,
as I have come to know
that life's journey is not a goal
but my unfolding self to grow.

The Simple

It's pure. It's basic. It's undeniably sweet.
It's the mellow encounter; it's very discreet.
It's life at the center—the original plan,
made to be simple, not the complexity of man.

How do we fall into the trap of confusion?
Is it stress as we obsess over the illusion
that life is meant to be struggle and strain,
to be filled with anxiety, judgment, and pain?

Release these intentions; it doesn't have to be.
Retrain your brain to live happily and free.
Step off that mountain, and soar unencumbered.
Your entire life can be filled with awe and wonder.

The secret of life is defined by the One—
to embrace truth and enjoy the simplicity of fun.
It's the element of the simple that we may come to find,
to redefine the basics in the love and life of humankind.

———————

DAILY DECLARATION OF EMPOWERMENT
THE SIMPLE

IN THE LIGHT OF MY SOUL, I DECLARE:

Today, I keep it simple.
I act without acting,
as the way to do is to be.

Light

I am the light of my truth,
as it is the way of the Way.
It is the call of being
to be acknowledged each new day.

It is in the unspoken word,
where the radiance of inner light shines.
It is all in what you have heard
with lovingness and Truth Divine.

The message of light is yours ...

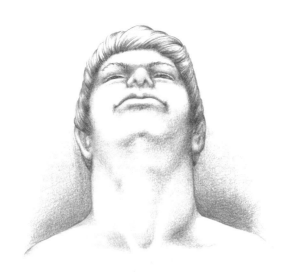

DAILY DECLARATION OF EMPOWERMENT
LIGHT
In the light of my soul, I declare:

I am the light of Truth; it is the way of the Way.
It is the love of being, acknowledged each new day.

50

Listen

Listen to the call of nature
from the forest's floor—
blades of grass conversing, dancing,
growing evermore.
Gently nestle into the bedlike grass, relax,
feel free;
softly close your eyes, be silent,
just listen and see.

Your mental and emotional being
create pictures within;
it is your spiritual Essence
that hears the drop of a pin.
Learn to use discernment
as you go deep into relaxation;
eliminate expectation,
and simply be with all creation.

If you choose to pray
to the Source of your being,
you are willingly talking;
there is no seeing.
As you deliberately enter
into a relaxed and calm state,
you open your inner ears for a still, quiet voice—
patiently wait.

Courageously journey down
your life's path to find
that it is straight and narrow;
it doesn't deviate or wind.
It is in the nature of knowingness
that makes it simple, not complex.
Feel and sense the impression within;
listen for guidance next.

Feel the lush grass around you,
the breeze massaging your face.
Know when truth is upon thee,
you will be filled with Grace.
The realization of oneness
is an illumination of the soul.
As the concept of yourself expands,
you will release all roles.

You will begin to let go of the labels
and roles you have taken on.
You will open yourself up to freely express
from a space far beyond.
Listen for truth in your heart;
the gift of unfoldment is yours.
The Dominion expresses through Spirit;
it lovingly opens doors.

Listen with your inner ears now.
Get silent, and go inside.
Await the communion of truth;
within you it peacefully resides.
Be patient, love yourself, fill yourself up
with respect and compassion.
The expression of truth reveals itself
in right time and right action.

DAILY DECLARATION OF EMPOWERMENT
LISTEN

IN THE LIGHT OF MY SOUL, I DECLARE:

I listen and feel truth in my heart;
this gift of revealing is mine.
Angelic Dominion expresses;
inner doorways open in time.

I listen. I trust. I act. I am.

Clarity

This poem is meant for you
as I hold you in my mind.
I realize your thoughts are racing
as you search to seek or find,
that clarity in seeing is masked
by the world of form,
of what we've grown to know as societal
and cultural norms.

Although your will expresses weakness
by the gripping vultures of past,
please make the conscious choice to break
patterns; they don't have to last.
Fear is the greatest obstacle
to clarity in your life.
Listen to your inner teacher. Free yourself;
eliminate the strife.

Create the vision in your mind
of exactly what you desire—
even though this is ego-based,
it will ignite your inner fire.
To reach deep down to the core of being,
your Essence graciously speaks;
through your personality, it recognizes
all you'll find as you seek.

Clarify your purpose now; embrace
the cavern's depth inside.
It is all you are in this unconditional love
by which you truly abide.
Surrender, release, accept what was—
it is time to be *all* you.
It is in this knowingness of clarity
you will find the greatest gift:
you!

DAILY DECLARATION OF EMPOWERMENT
CLARITY

IN THE LIGHT OF MY SOUL, I DECLARE:

I clarify my purpose now, digging deep from the inside.
I live a life of surrender and love by which I truly abide.

Forgiveness

Forgiveness is a word
I truthfully extol,
releasing emotional attachment,
awakening reality of my soul.

Forgiveness delivers my shielded heart
far beyond its norm,
uplifting beingness from judgment, doubt,
how to conform.

The reality of forgiveness
is a knowing I do find:
the essence of my being,
pureness of heart and mind.

I forgive myself and others now,
for it is of the past.
I unlock the hold of relentless thought;
I willingly out cast.

The heart of forgiveness lovingly
disintegrates illusions of old
while my faith in the moment's light
guides peace and love to unfold.

As I forgive, I surrender
to the highest of Thee,
freeing myself to gain clarity
in the vision of what is to be.

As I now forgive, the nature
of balance settles within my core.
I neutralize life's ebb and flow,
accepting myself forevermore.

———————

DAILY DECLARATION OF EMPOWERMENT
FORGIVENESS

IN THE LIGHT OF MY SOUL, I DECLARE:

I forgive myself and others now, for it is of the past.
As I forgive, I free myself to live.

Angel Wings

It is sometimes difficult to recognize
the one with elegant wings,
the kind that when outstretched,
embrace the heavens that sing.
These wings glide freely
in the breeze of Divine Grace,
soaring, floating, suspended
in the magnificence of infinite space.

The wings of an angel display
great honor and trust;
they encourage love and harmony
to all with a must.
The wings of an angel will gently guide you
through your day
as you learn to be accepting,
knowing the answer is in the Way.

The angels want your goodness
to be expressed from your core.
Now trust in their guidance
rather than question what they are for.
The wings of an angel will offer you a lesson,
not a free ride,
to practice flying freely
after grasping the toss of a turbulent tide.

An angel is filled with lightheartedness,
laughter, and fun.
Smile with your angels, and recognize
your connectedness to the One.
It is in the guidance of your angels
as you come to know
that you are an angel too, learning
and yearning to grow.

Can you take your angel wings
and spread them open wide
to allow the Essence of yourself,
the core of being inside—
to reveal your truth and expression
that uniquely is you
through the angelic realm of illumination,
brilliant and new?

———————

DAILY DECLARATION OF EMPOWERMENT
ANGEL WINGS

IN THE LIGHT OF MY SOUL, I DECLARE:

I feel the wings of my angel gently guiding me this day
as I learn to be accepting, knowing the answer is in Way.

Surrender

Energy stirs in my core to awaken
the sleep-filled dark—
a grand illumination, a self-realization,
recognizing my angel's hark.
I encounter deep trust to let go
and reveal what is erupting in me,
to free myself of guilt and fear,
the root system I clearly see.

My depths of knowingness loosen within
for conditions to release.
I acknowledge the emotions as they surface,
honor them, and feel peace.
Sometimes, I make the choice to feel it again,
forgive myself, and be
open in my heart, free in mind,
my spirit available to be all of me.

I am all that I am, lovingly connected
to universal Source,
expanding conscious awareness,
sharing my true course.
As I surrender and forgive,
I detach and rise above.
I embrace serenity and freedom now,
the truth of unconditional love.

———

DAILY DECLARATION OF EMPOWERMENT
SURRENDER

IN THE LIGHT OF MY SOUL, I DECLARE:

I surrender and forgive; I detach and rise above.
I embrace freedom in the truth of unconditional love.

Lighthearted

Lift it, open it, light it up—free yourself to soar.
Expand your heart in spontaneity; leap as you explore.
Feel the gentle heart of the playful child inside,
expressing laughter in the cheer to seek or to hide.

Lightheartedness is being lifted in a light, fun way
like the luminescent rising sun of each new day.
As you awaken to the presence of lightness, fresh and free,
be lovingly and consciously aware for all of you to be.

You can lightly break the patterns of days and years past.
Open yourself to expansiveness, sheer balance, and the vast.
You are filled with light and laughter in your happy heart,
bathing in the moment's space, releasing associations in parts.

Reach high, and stretch yourself, grasping a cloud above.
Pull yourself up; float freely as you fly with the white dove.
Feel the lightness of your life with an unencumbered sense,
granting yourself possibilities, being
relaxed rather than tense.

With this peaceful, light heart comes great compassion.
Share your virtues with others, guiding
their conscious action.
You are this lighthearted being as
you express from your core
that nothing matters but right now, no less or no more.

Pay attention to the lightness in each
present moment today,
freeing yourself from limited living, expanding how you may.
Lightheartedness has always been an integral part of you.
Express your heart lightly; transform
the old you into the new.

———————

DAILY DECLARATION OF EMPOWERMENT
LIGHTHEARTED

IN THE LIGHT OF MY SOUL, I DECLARE:

I willingly free myself of limited living,
expanding lightheartedly how I may.

Inner Guidance

Be all that you are;
it is not hard to be.
The distance may seem far,
but you are really ready to be free.

Your inner guidance is there for you;
get silent, and go within.
Be prepared for change through and through;
trust and believe it is a win-win.

These messages will continue to come
as you prepare for your life's work.
It will provide support and encourage which from
denial and suppression may lurk.

That's all for now; as you can see,
the message is quite clear.
You must persist and reveal the *me*
and release every bit of fear.

Yes, you are on your way now
for others to watch from afar.
Stay centered as in the way of the Dao,
and you will teach people who you really are.

DAILY DECLARATION OF EMPOWERMENT
INNER GUIDANCE

IN THE LIGHT OF MY SOUL, I DECLARE:

I am one with my inner guidance, silent and focused within.
I trust my confident steadiness, reframing any chaotic spin.

Inner Life

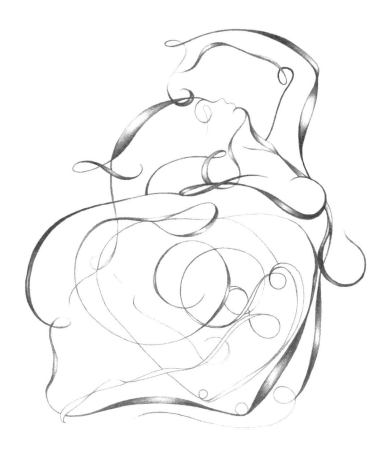

An extraordinary sensation filters
through the body-mind so pure,
rushing from the toe to head—
connecting the dimensions, as it were.
A heightened knowing, an inner rhythm
coupled deep and beyond—
part of the gentle consciousness
of love and light so fond.

The presence of oneness engulfs each cell,
emerging, expanding within,
a transmutation of body and mind,
releasing impartation in.
This state of being is lifted above
the human world of thought,
purely one global song,
a liberating expression caught.

Be in the plenitude of Grace,
streaming far and free,
renewing your oneness with every aspect
of you and me to Thee.
The healing blessing bestowed upon your heart,
your soul, and mind
integrates in stillness as you detach
from thought of any kind.

The instantaneous moment
is enlightened through your trust,
communing in the blissful essence,
free of should or must.
Let go the world of thought
to open yourself to be,
expanding your sense of self with the Source
in all of Thee.

The rhythm of the inner life flourishes
beyond time and space,
free of projection in mind, living truth
from the heart in Grace.

––––––––––––

DAILY DECLARATION OF EMPOWERMENT
INNER LIFE

IN THE LIGHT OF MY SOUL, I DECLARE:

The rhythm of my inner life flourishes beyond time and space.
I release rigid concepts, embodying empowered Grace.

Be and Receive

It is in the gift of receiving that we come to know
that love embraces us fully as we allow ourselves to grow.
To receive is to be accepting, sincere, and truly humble.
Open your arms to all! Cease the fumble in the tumble.

As you share your light through the windows of your being,
allow others to give to you to enhance and enlighten your seeing.
Your path is paved in clarity as you allow it all to unfold.
Hold on to your truth, for your Essence will be told.

It is in the gift of receiving that we learn how to share,
to give from the heart without a question or a dare.
It is time for your awareness to direct itself in truth.
You are whole in yourself now. Watch the unveiling—it's the proof.

————

DAILY DECLARATION OF EMPOWERMENT
BE AND RECEIVE

IN THE LIGHT OF MY SOUL, I DECLARE:

I embrace the gift of receiving with an open heart this day.
My soul spreads its wings, expanding every which way.

Balance

It is in the midpoint of opposites
that we gain perspective to view
our lives as visions of wholeness
that are peaceful, healthy, and new.

Through the principle of duality,
can we truly come to learn
the creativeness in our realities
as we teeter, totter, and turn?

The midpoint of opposites is balance
as we search in the to and fro,
engaging in life's mystical dance
to embrace what our spirits truly know.

It is not in the *either-or* thought
or the *neither-this-nor-that* thinking
that we experience the space of neutrality,
creating upliftment, keeping us from sinking.

You will find in this space of freedom
a life crystalized in clarity and bliss
to discover the gentle balance of life from
unfoldment of wholeness that is neither
that nor this.

———————————

DAILY DECLARATION OF EMPOWERMENT
BALANCE

IN THE LIGHT OF MY SOUL, I DECLARE:

I recognize the midpoint of balance
is a search in the to and the fro,
engaging in life's mystical dance,
embracing what my spirit truly knows.

It Is What It Is

The moment of truth is captured
in the unspoken word.
It is revealed from the heart—
intrinsically felt, not heard.
This knowingness is embellished
upon the consciousness walls,
expressing the impression
of reality's hidden falls.

So difficult it is to escape
illusions here and now.
Accept the knowledge of inner guidance:
release, expand, allow.
The voice of reason may temptingly alter
your decision to act;
yet the allowance of the unspoken word jousts
with brilliant tact.

A-ha! You project from your
love-sustaining heart
the magnificence of rightness acknowledged
from the start.
The windows of the eyes
see the truth as it is.
It cannot hide the essence of the soul;
it is what it is.

DAILY DECLARATION OF EMPOWERMENT
IT IS WHAT IT IS

IN THE LIGHT OF MY SOUL, I DECLARE:

I realize life lessons reveal for me to see
that it is what it is, as it is to be.

Honor

Pause for a moment to recognize
the space in your heart—
that which represents respect, reflecting
the greater sum of parts.
This deep respect conveys acceptance
of the self with love;
it awakens to a higher sense of awareness
from above.

To honor from above, below, outside,
and all around,
it starts from the heart, the essence
so profound.
Take a step within yourself, and feel
the greatness in
the expansiveness of your soul,
the infinite therein.

Take a ride on the wings of glory, floating,
gliding free.
Claim the goodness in your heart,
owning, honoring Thee.
Open yourself, be more aware, experience
magnificence now.
Opportunity is awaiting you—honor it,
lovingly allow.

Honor your body, your soul,
and your mind;
a vision of balance and harmony
you will find.
Bring forth from within a spark
of your being.
Honor your inner guidance, a reflection
of your seeing.

Honor all that you are;
rest in contemplation.
Reach and touch the brightest star;
embrace the elation.
You are deserving of all the love
buried in your soul.
Accept, respect, and honor this—
it's your birthright, not a goal.

IN THE LIGHT OF MY SOUL, I DECLARE:

I am deserving of all the love emanating in my soul.
I accept, respect, and honor this as my birthright, not a goal.

Gateway 3

The Unconditioned Self

COME TO BE

There is no need to run outside for better seeing,
nor to peer from a window.
Rather abide at the center of your being,
for the more you leave it, the less you learn.
Search your heart and see,
if s/he is wise who takes each turn,
the way to do is to be.
—Lao Zi, *Dao De Jing*

Awaken to the realization that all is Spirit, and in Spirit, there is no disharmony. Here, you live as your True Self. You have let go of the dream or illusion of what you thought you were, to truly be all that you are in your essence. Now, when Truth is spoken, recognize it as the Essence of all, the One being, the realization of the unity of God, the Universe, the Infinite, and humankind. This is Truth. To commune in the stillness of silence is to reach your hand forth and lift yourself up to this knowingness. It is light. It is love. It is knowledge. It is presence. It is all that you are in all that you are. Your intellect does not heal you; only the integrative union of your soul being and your personal being heals.

The Essence of all is omnipotent, omniscient, and omnipresent. We are one in this great field of Essence. Just be in it. Be still, and be in the Essence of wholeness and the oneness therein. In this process, we evolve into the light of understanding and become spiritually awakened.

THE UNCONDITIONED SELF

- experiences Divine universal presence
- lives in the eternal present moment
- accepts and trusts the highest good for all
- envisions a more enlightened global consciousness for all sentient beings
- lovingly holds up the world, consciously assisting humanity in its healing process
- experiences limitless potential and boundless radiant essence of One-Self
- accepts that change is our only constant
- prayerfully blesses the world in peace, love, goodwill, and solidarity
- contemplates, meditates, practices internal cultivation, and cultivates spiritual discernment
- stands strong and steady in the light of the soul

the self realized

Transformation

To seek personal transformation
is manifesting change within.
Carefully consider all parts of being;
then proceed to go in.
Initiating this course of action
is acknowledgement at your core.
You realize you are more than human;
step through the ethereal door.

To change oneself is to honor all that resides
in the depths of being.
Refocus from the outer world toward
the inner sense of seeing.
This place of all knowing is the divine, intuitive
spiritual home
from which we walked away,
independently on the roam.

No need to search any longer,
for truth is beating in your heart.
It has always danced with your beingness
right from the start.
The truth is you as this spiritual being,
awaiting the journey back.
Embrace the Essence of All That Is,
grasping the eternal track.

You will transform your mental
and emotional self, physical being too.
Own all that you are right now
as you lovingly release to renew.
Conditioned patterns lose power;
the ego's purpose no longer is in view.
The secret of life's happiness
has always been with you.

When the unfoldment of truth
tenderly guides you through the gate,
it is your spirit lovingly exclaiming
it is never too late.
This is the journey, the inner path
you've discovered deep in your core.
Share this knowingness with others now;
be in your all-ness forevermore.

––––––––––––

DAILY DECLARATION OF EMPOWERMENT
TRANSFORMATION

IN THE LIGHT OF MY SOUL, I DECLARE:

I am transforming my mental and emotional self,
my physical being too.
I own all that I am
as I lovingly release to renew.

To Be

The nature of wholeness
is in the learning to be;
it is in the present moment
as we use discernment to see.

The gracious gift of the Essence of all
reveals in the now
as we lovingly, patiently
await to allow—

to allow the omniscient, still voice
of the blessed guidance within
bestow upon our beingness
peace and love deep in.

Thus, *being* is the Divine life
of heaven here on earth;
unfolding in the process is our expansion
of self, service, and worth.

Lao Zi eloquently expressed,
"The way to do is to be,"
kindling our inner beingness to forgive,
be truth-filled, feel free.

Once we harken to the state of beingness
in our every day,
the act of doing will gently follow
in a unified, harmonic way.

To be is to release the intention
of any wrong or right,
holding in our hearts the present stillness
of the light.

To be is to dissolve association
in the laws of duality,
recognizing the Spirit in all,
love's arms embracing reality.

So it is in the realm of being
that lifts our hearts and souls
to be liberated in a timeless reality,
detached from the drama of control.

———————

DAILY DECLARATION OF EMPOWERMENT
TO BE

IN THE LIGHT OF MY SOUL, I DECLARE:

I abide at the center of my being
as I search my heart to see.
Through the inner gateway,
I enter the way to do is to be.

Awareness Rising

No matter how difficult it may seem
to acknowledge who you are,
remember the roots from whence you came—
eternity is now, not afar.

Your spiritual beingness is yearning
to be recognized by all of you,
to have you embrace the depth of your soul
and say to the highest, "Yes, I do."

Do you recognize your soul and connectedness
to the generous One
to respect and honor the healing art
of all daughters and sons?

Conscious awareness is rising
as you lift your essence to speak,
knowing the Divine and the One
are all a part of the courageous and meek.

Trust with your heart as you expand your sense
of all that you are.
It is in the powerful, loving moment you are
guided by the light's luminescent star.

Release the conditions that pull you in,
resisting the thought of change.
Allow the brilliance of Essence
as you joyfully lift and arrange.

To detach from the old patterns
as you create newness far in
is to believe the truth of reality,
as your existence is not about sin.

For sin is an earthly creation
that was given power to.
Now it is time to change the moment,
to love and share through and through.

Yes, it is the simple plan,
as it was meant to be,
to move through what is necessary for you,
and then you will agree.

Your conscious awareness is rising
as your level of spirituality shines.
Now share your truth with others
as you renew the hope in Thine.

DAILY DECLARATION OF EMPOWERMENT
AWARENESS RISING

IN THE LIGHT OF MY SOUL, I DECLARE:

Conscious awareness is rising
as my level of spirituality shines.
I share my essence with others
to renew hope in the sacred human design.

Unfoldment

Unfoldment is the gentle whisper
of infinite God guiding you.
It is the silent knowingness of how to act,
what to do.
The action comes from the message
far and deep within.
Only you can recognize it if you are mindful
as you go in.

The tendency to direct your own course
and make a human choice
disregards the essence of unfoldment delivered
from the inner voice.
The difference from intellectual reasoning
and unfolding deep inside
is the security of conditioned thought,
not the trust of your inner guide.

I know it may seem difficult to make sense
of this at first.
Free your mind of conditioned patterns;
allow yourself to thirst.
Open yourself up freely to the meaning
of all that you are.
Feel yourself—indulge in the moment's brilliance;
you will reach far.

Do not be afraid of the gloriousness
that is part of you.
Allow yourself to experience the present,
a vision clear and new.
It is trust and patience in the unfolding process
here on earth,
guided through the ethereal heavens planted
in your soul at birth.

Yes, you can acknowledge the grandness
of all you truly are.
Believe, have faith, release the doubt,
reveal your radiant star.
When it is unfolded unto you,
follow the lead of the light.
You will be humbly awakened,
embracing inner peace and inner sight.

DAILY DECLARATION OF EMPOWERMENT
UNFOLDMENT

IN THE LIGHT OF MY SOUL, I DECLARE:

Unfoldment is the gentle whisper of infinite God,
loving and true.
It is the silent knowingness
as I trust how to act and what to do.

I Miss You

The sadness swells in my body
as I allow the tears to release.
I realize my friend's spirit
is soaring freely this moment in peace.

I sigh. I let go; I cry.
I do whatever impresses my heart.
I see. I feel; I know.
Essence of Spirit guides me as it imparts.

I incarnate. I live; I rebirth,
time and time again.
I evolve in my Essence,
seeking wisdom and mastery to ascend.

I anchor into the Truth of Spirit,
unconsciously relaxing my breath.
I fear not the transition of life,
the unfolding process of death.

I cannot help my thoughts of you
as I reach out my hands to feel,
to acknowledge your presence,
which is gone, no longer physically real.

I lovingly hold your memory in my mind
as my heart gallantly adjusts to the new.
I carry on in the moments light
as I'm surrounded in an angelic, white healing hue.

I miss you. Soar freely.

───────────

DAILY DECLARATION OF EMPOWERMENT
I MISS YOU

IN THE LIGHT OF MY SOUL, I DECLARE:

I anchor into the Truth of Spirit, unconsciously relaxing my breath.
I fear not the transition of life, the unfolding process of death.

Compassionate Detachment

In the loving embrace of Spirit,
we mend the heart of its fear.
In it is the Divine rightness
as we release the relentless past years.

As we open ourselves to unfoldment,
we see Truth in the eyes of Grace.
It is this compassionate detachment
that heals and renews our inner space.

From this place of transformative rebirth,
a new perspective flourishes in thee,
gleaned from the loving detachment of
what was honorable—a part of me.

Through our insightful acknowledgement,
we have gained a vision to see
that our compassionate detachment is
about self-acceptance and respect
as we lovingly set ourselves free.

———————

DAILY DECLARATION OF EMPOWERMENT
COMPASSIONATE DETACHMENT

IN THE LIGHT OF MY SOUL, I DECLARE:

I willingly embrace unfoldment.
I see truth in the eyes of Grace;
it is compassionate detachment
healing and renewing my inner space.

Suspend Yourself and Relax

Suspend yourself in the buoyant blue waters,
floating on the edge with ease.
Embrace upon your face the peaceful massage,
the healing effect of the breeze.
Give into gravity, relax deep in
as your mind and body lie adrift.
Feel the release; trust in the waters,
the acceptance and support of this gift.

It is the beauty of the waters absorbed
through your loving and clear essence
that creates a harmonic convergence,
enlightening your true presence.
As the melodious rhythm of nature's way
lulls you far and beyond,
a simultaneous flow in communion
generates inner joy so fond.

Embrace this place through unfoldment
suspended in you so free—
the awakening of your true self
honoring and accepting all of thee.

Relax ...

DAILY DECLARATION OF EMPOWERMENT
SUSPEND YOURSELF AND RELAX

IN THE LIGHT OF MY SOUL, I DECLARE;

I imagine I am one with the melodious rhythm of nature
lulling me far and beyond.
I am grounded in the flow of communion,
generating inner joy oh so profound.

Communion with Thee

Oh, Divine Spirit, you lovingly placed
in our minds to see
that all of life's lessons bring us back
to be with Thee.

Oh, Divine Spirit, you purely placed
in our hearts to feel,
challenging our awareness to know
what is illusion and what is real.

You have given us the opportunity
to be in conflict at the ego's request,
to experience the mesmerizing state
of the delusional self, the obsessed.

To be in Your love is to embrace truth,
compassion, and the One,
releasing the control and power
of the little self on the run.

We stand away to serenely observe
the life that we lead,
to allow ourselves tranquil living
as we plant the simplicity seed.

The perceptions from the ego-base
are tainted from conditions past,
continuing the whirlwind drama of illusion.
How long will this last?

Interpretations are the ego's powerful grip
on the mind,
strangling our vision of reality and love
of nature and the kind.

To be all that we are
is to awaken to Your pure love,
built into our genetic code,
linked to You within and above.

We shan't take this message lightly,
for it is time to be whole,
acknowledging our essence,
releasing the past, freeing our holy souls.

We are intuitively guided to start fresh now.
The cause is for us to see,
that it is about our connection with All,
for us to be in communion with Thee.

DAILY DECLARATION OF EMPOWERMENT
COMMUNION WITH THEE

IN THE LIGHT OF MY SOUL, I DECLARE:

I am intuitively guided to start fresh today.
The cause is for me to see
that I am in communion with Thee.

I Am

I Am the breath you take in as you fill your core with Grace.

I Am the light of heaven drawing illumination to your face.

I Am the beautiful eagle soaring strongly across the skies.

I Am the fury in the heart of the lonely one who cries.

I Am the narrow vision stretching itself to expand.

I Am the meager fallacy searching for truth so grand.

I Am the lesson in everything—
opportunity to listen and learn.

I Am the vibrant reality as you unfold with every turn.

I Am the lavender-laced mountain; upon
me, you awaken with awe.

I Am the knowingness reflected through
the eyes you longingly saw.

I Am the lifted presence you felt as you were so still.

I Am the Truth of All. I Am acknowledged
through your free will.

I Am all that I Am. I Am the light of your truth.

I Am the Essence of all, a life of love you live as my proof.

I Am.

DAILY DECLARATION OF EMPOWERMENT
I AM

IN THE LIGHT OF MY SOUL, I DECLARE:

I Am all that I Am. I Am the light of Truth.
I am one with the Essence of all,
a life of love I live as pure proof. I Am.

The Essence of Spirit

Elaborate textures reveal themselves as you sift
through the rough and the pure,
elevating your awareness to recognize the
pious posture's allure.
Brilliance lives within your heart to be awakened
in the moment's light.
It is your generous, illumined self making the
dark sunshine bright.

It is the nature of wholeness that speaks from
your individual soul
in the search for communion with Spirit,
the Truth, and embracing your role.
Your vision gets blurred by the illusion of
dragons in the night.
Although they appear to be in dream state,
always seek out the light.

It is the Spirit of all filling you with
dignity, grace, and love.
You must recognize, intuit, and feel what
is or isn't from above.
It is in the gentle knowingness that we
guide you from deep in.
It is your alert perception that is felt
as if razor-thin.

The light and the way are provided to you
as you journey long and far.
Deliverance in the Essence of Spirit is your
eternal gift and guiding star.
As you awaken to the message that "I Am
forever the light of your Truth,"
you will understand betrayal of the fittest
and the loyalty and love as my proof.

Allow the warmth and tender surround of
Grace's wings so free
to lovingly engage themselves as they lift
and honor all of Thee.
Secure and special, the message of Truth
falls upon all of you,
cultivating and creating clarity, a vision
of what you are to do.

The light, the Truth, the Essence of Spirit
that I Am directing your hand,
releasing the pull of gravity, expanding
consciousness in every grain of sand—
open your heart, and feel the reminder of love's dew
caress your lip.
You will taste and feel the greatness in the
reality of this life's trip.

———————

DAILY DECLARATION OF EMPOWERMENT
THE ESSENCE OF SPIRIT

IN THE LIGHT OF MY SOUL, I DECLARE:

I breathe deep the Essence of Spirit,
the sound of silence—
radiant, boundless, and whole.

Feel the Flow of Spirit

The veils of illusion appear impermeable
as we blindly find our way
to the knowing reality underneath
the external conditioned day.

As we step outside ourselves to serenely
observe true presence,
our awareness is awakened by the
claimed belief of lack and absence.

Conscious awareness rises as we pursue
our realization of the all,
journeying deep within ourselves,
guided in the search after the fall.

As we fell away from the Essence of all
that we were to be,
we've become enlightened to the ancient
wisdom that we are a part of Thee.

To dance in the Essence of oneness is a
glorifying, mystifying waltz—
flowing in the fluidity of Truth, releasing
seduction of the false.

Embrace now, and sense the impression,
the God-realization in the still.
Feel and absorb this knowingness
at the core of your own will.

Realize mental thoughts cannot bring
forth the communing of all;
it is in the loving acknowledgment of
unfoldment in the Truth of your call.

As you resist the ego-thought that there is
only one way to see,
rightness and knowingness are the alchemy
of awareness for you to truly be.

So expand your concept of self as you
open your heart to feel
that the flow of Spirit in communion is not justified;
it's a knowingness that is real.

———————

DAILY DECLARATION OF EMPOWERMENT
FEEL THE FLOW OF SPIRIT

IN THE LIGHT OF MY SOUL, I DECLARE:

As I release any ego thought
that there is only one way to see,
I realize the alchemy of awareness
is for me to truly be.

I flow with Spirit.

Pure Love

Love is a knowing energy that we share as we
open our guarded hearts to be.

Love is a quenched thirst that continues to flow
unobstructed and carefree.

Love carries the light of the heart
to enliven the Spirit in humankind.

Love encourages the hopeless as they discover
brilliance in their body and mind.

Love dances deep in as it awakens
an intention to be filled.

Love expands our awareness to the limitless
potential we are willed.

Love is steeped in gratitude, for our
exchange seems so unreal—

To touch, to taste, to go beyond that
which expresses what we feel.

Love is a knowledge, an unfiltered wisdom
untouched by human error.

It acknowledges our innocence and invulnerability
as we unconditionally care.

Love is the Divine knowing that we are
here to be

One in the same, hand in hand, reaching to
the highest degree.

Love is pure. Love is the supreme flow of energy
unencumbered in motion and bliss.

It has no limits because it is the
great Source of pure beingness.

Love:
Be it. Give it. Receive it. Allow it.

Allow love's compassion to permeate
every cell of the whole and feel it.

Just get in touch with the heart center's
flutter in the rush of love's pure tide.

It expands the synchronous moment into stillness,
a trust-filled knowing we abide.

So the dainty trickle of a succulent dewdrop
moistens the earth with love;

It continues to share its delight to bare
its essence from nature above.

Yes, love is nature, an energy,
an unknowable, unified presence.

Love is you through and through.
It is your true essence—

pure love.

DAILY DECLARATION OF EMPOWERMENT
PURE LOVE

IN THE LIGHT OF MY SOUL, I DECLARE:

Love is the supreme flow of energy
unencumbered in motion and bliss.

It has no limits because it is the
great Source of pure being-ness.

I am love, and I am loved.

The Moon

Moon so bright,
An incredible sight—
Jewel so high,
Majesty of sky.

Drift far away;
Bathe in the rays.
Energy moving through
Creates change anew.

How to describe
The feeling that resides
Deep in my heart,
Nurturing all parts?

A healing illumination,
An earthly creation
Delivering its essence—
A mystifying presence.

Gaze into space,
Galaxy in place.
Take yourself home:
Dream, wander, roam.

DAILY DECLARATION OF EMPOWERMENT
THE MOON

IN THE LIGHT OF MY SOUL, I DECLARE:

I drift far away, bathing in her rays.
I embody her vibration.
I ground the change.
I release. I manifest. I co-create. I Am.

Believe Me
When I Say I Am

Believe me when I say
I am feeling the world's despair.
Believe me when I say
I am discovering that many do care.

Believe me when I say
I am envisioning a world of love.
Believe me when I say
I am crystalizing inner strength from above.

Believe me when I say
I am praying for world peace.
Believe me when I say
I am encouraging people to release.

Believe me when I say
I am enlightened by your gaze.
Believe me when I say
I am touched by your ways.

Believe me when I say
I am revealing my inner Essence.
Believe me when I say
I am acknowledging your true presence.

Believe me when I say
I am searching from inside myself.
Believe me when I say
I am visioning for everyone's good health.

Believe me when I say
I am teaching from my heart.
Believe me when I say
I am trying to finish what I start.

Believe me when I say
I am guided by the Spirit of all.
Believe me when I say
I am confident to learn from the fall.

Believe me when I say
I am living in the angels' glow.
Believe me when I say
I am harmonizing with all I truly know.

———————

DAILY DECLARATION OF EMPOWERMENT
BELIEVE ME WHEN I SAY I AM

IN THE LIGHT OF MY SOUL, I DECLARE:

Believe me when I say
I am living in my angels' glow,
flowing in the wisdom stream,
harmonizing with all I truly know.

The Nature of God

The luminescent sun appears,
cresting the canyon wall,
projecting upon the red sandstone
its expansive image so tall.

Convoluted structures of magnificent stone
so strong
surround the water's edge as fish dance
and birds hymn their sweet song.

As I sit afloat in the water,
centered in the canyon's delight,
the vision of what I see can only be measured
by God's insight.

This masterful creation has evolved
from the highest indeed,
its magnificence a revelation of a peace-filled
moment planted as a seed.

I listen to love's echo resonate deep
in these beauteous walls.
Lauded in all its holiness, I embrace Truth,
the essence of God's call.

––––––––––––––

DAILY DECLARATION OF EMPOWERMENT
THE NATURE OF GOD

IN THE LIGHT OF MY SOUL, I DECLARE:

I listen to love's echo
resonate deep within nature's walls,
lauded in all its holiness,
the essence of Mother/Father God's call.

The attainment of the
mountainous summit is to
discover the True Self.

AFTERWORD

You may find synthesizing this information feels natural to you, or it may be a struggle. Either way you look at it, it has stimulated a shift in your consciousness. You may have begun to experience a more open, nonjudgmental awareness. You may have begun to acknowledge the present moment as the sweet nectar of life that it is. You may have found that you are not getting caught up in the mundane or trivial, recognizing it as a mere blip in all of reality. You may have found your mirror reflection in a friend with whom you have made a deep connection. You may even have found yourself embracing the beauty of the butterfly's symmetry in flight or being awestruck by the sight of a lavender-laced mountainscape.

The shift in your consciousness will graduate you to new heights. You may own the realization that you are an incredible being, spiritually and humanly balanced and aligned with your divine nature and human nature as one. The radiance of your light and essence reveals itself as you completely accept your goodness free from conditions. You may have found that loving detachment through trust and faith will carry you lightly through the ethereal gateway. Perhaps the neutral space between opposites has given you a new sense of freedom, unity, spontaneity, unification, equality, harmony, and love. With the lessons learned and more to come, you have elevated your self-awareness, listening with inner ears and seeing with inner eyes. Applying life lessons into daily living is about uniting your outer and inner world. As you continue to challenge the shadowy corners of self, your spiritual discernment will become more refined.

Contemplate the poems as you need. Glance at them as guideposts, or completely immerse yourself in them. Ask a question you have been contemplating, or simply request guidance in the day and then gently flip through the pages to find your landing point. Equally enjoy creating and using your own crafted cutout declaration cards at the back of the book. Bless them, shuffle them, and select the declaration that directs you to the poem and the harmonization of its verse. You will receive the divine energetic resonance encoded in the verse, woven within the sacred sound stream to enlighten your true self. Recite the daily declarations as seeds of truth that are vibrationally connected to the poetic verse. They will set the tone of intention to elicit deeper awakening and expansion into the full expression of all that you are and have always been from the beginning of time.

Your intuitive self will continue to expand as you make space within to grow. Empty out so that you may be filled. There is no right or wrong in it; it just is. You will continue to make choices, learn life lessons, and expand your awareness, realizing your oneness in the web of life, the interconnectedness of all things.

The words, the verse, and the energy within this book are for soulfully enhancing your conscious awareness to embody your nature of being whole in body, mind, heart, and soul. If I have touched you in a somewhat curious, mystical way, then I am sincerely grateful for sharing my experiences with you. If you find that you are unaffected by the contents of this book, I am grateful for that too. Everything serves a higher purpose, as our life paths direct us in perfect synchronicity. Wherever you are on your path, accept, honor, forgive, and love yourself unconditionally. The Source of your being is gently guiding your hand. Just reach inside, climb your inner mountain, and live from your Essence, poised in presence, embracing the nature of being whole.

Key Concepts

Affirmation: A personal, positive statement, written in the present tense (as if it has occurred), that embodies a purpose or a goal. When repeated several times, these directed energies of positive thought will reprogram the conscious mind. Affirmations are used to balance and heal the emotional and mental body.

Angelic: Referring to the kingdom of angels, which is unlike the human kingdom in that angels are invisible. They serve to manifest Divine impression through human form. This realm guides, directs, and compassionately unfolds an intelligent deliverance of universal wisdom as messengers of the Essence of All/God.

Atonement: At-one-ment is the state of oneness reflecting unity and harmony in humankind and universal Source.

Attachment: The hidden vice of the ego that holds tight to the illusion of form. This illusion creates a thick veil over the eyes and heart to inhibit insight. Right thought, acceptance, and forgiveness encourage illumination, thus loving detachment of the thoughtform.

Beingness: The full state of being; the encompassing of all Essence; accepting and honoring all that is around and throughout the self.

Centered: A state of inner balance merging the physical, emotional, mental, and spiritual bodies in wellbeing.

Compassion: The synthesized aspect of wisdom and love, unconditionally delivered.

Consciousness: Mind with knowledge. Consciousness is the combined result of the intellect and matter integrated and synthesized into a focused awareness. To expand the sense of consciousness is to know within oneself what cannot be physically recognized—a subjective recognition of subtle truth and intuitive awareness.

Contemplation: Using the mind to hold steady a mental device, such as a word or thoughtform, and then serenely observing the unlimited possibilities; simply being in the present moment, watching with inner eyes, and listening with inner ears.

Detachment: Freeing ourselves from the hidden voice of the ego that is holding tight to the illusion of form. Through right thinking, acceptance, and forgiveness, loving detachment removes the veils that inhibit insight, thus encouraging illumination.

Dis-ease: A sense of disharmony and fragmentation reflected in the lower self nature. This uncomfortable nature often creates stress-induced illness in any or all aspects of our bodies, physically, emotionally, and mentally.

Dominion: A higher order of angels commissioned to administer the will of God, the Essence of All That Is.

Ego: The personality self that, when disciplined, brings balance to the physical, emotional, and mental bodies. When unbalanced, the ego displays controlling, selfish qualities. These qualities are broken down and transformed into compassion and loving detachment as lessons are learned toward soul integration.

Emotional Body: The aspect of the lower self that energetically resides in the solar plexus. The drama and turmoil of this body can be calmed by breaking emotional cycles, attachments, and patterns, which balances the ego. Energy follows thought; thus, how we think affects how we feel, and how we feel affects our physical reality. (See *mental body* and *physical body*.)

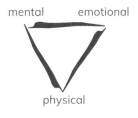

Energy: The vibration and frequency of invisible molecules of Essence coursing through all aspects of who we are and what we are, which makes up where we are; the unseen expression of all that we are connected to in the Nature of All Things.

Enlightenment: A state of mind filtered through the heart center, electrifying the entire sense of being and acknowledging a supreme knowing and wisdom.

Evolution of the Soul: The unfolding process toward a higher level of knowing and consciousness individually; the awakening of the human form to the reality of universal oneness through the plan of love, light, truth, and power.

Glamour: A distortion of perception induced by the desires of the emotional body that encourages the ego's need to control and manipulate. In the unfolding process of life's lessons, we dissipate our glamour and detach from the grip of our ego-based reality.

Grace: The spiritual showering of higher energies from the Essence of All/God/Goddess when a conscious shift has been made in one's level of knowingness and awareness. Grace is bestowed upon all who embrace the Essence of All That Is in the nature of all things.

Higher Self: The wise aspect of the higher self that guides you from the depths of your inner knowing when you listen with inner ears and see with inner eyes. (See *intuition* and *will of the soul.*)

will of the soul

higher self   intuition

I Am: Our identity with the presence of Spirit and the Godhead; the indwelling union of "I and the Father/Mother God/Universe are one"; the affirmation of "I Am all that I Am in all that I Am." I Am is a state of being— pure, unconditioned consciousness. We are one with the Essence of All That Is in our I Am presence.

Illumination: An insight based on self-realization that lights the path for greater clarity; one is illumined by a higher knowingness.

Illusions: Falsehoods of reality, typically dressed up as truth to trick the self as to what is and what isn't. Oftentimes, an illusion is a mask to our greater good perpetuated by a group of people with the same thoughtform, thus the statement "hypnotic state of the world."

Inner Guidance: The gentle, still voice within that always guides your hand and lights your path. Silence and stillness contribute to your ability to listen within; stress and drama inhibit your ability to feel your inner guidance.

Intuition: An aspect of the higher self that directs a higher level of consciousness beyond the rational mind. (See *higher self* and *will of the soul*.)

Mental Body: The aspect of the lower self that retains thought. The thought evolves as the mental body deconditions from its rigidly held beliefs and expands its awareness of the individual. In the process, illusions melt away, and clarity sets in. (See *physical body* and *emotional body*.)

Neutrality: The bridge with which the midpoint of opposites formulates a sense of balance, unity, freedom, and unification.

Physical Body: The aspect of the lower self that pertains to physical matter, through which the heart and soul are expressed. When ego/personality is unbalanced, the physical body displays symptoms of pain and tension. (See *mental body* and *emotional body*.)

Right Thinking: Thought can be constructive or destructive, creative or controlling; right thinking is about embracing the power of thought and directing it forth in right movement with right understanding of its subtle process.

Soul: The essence of the higher self that merges with the personality to form a balanced, whole sense of self. Our souls animate our physical forms. The soul is like a bridge, an interface between personality and Spirit. It expands the conscious level of our being within the realm of all possibilities.

Spirit: Breath; the universal breath of all of life; the Essence of nature's cosmic energetic connection; the breath of universal Essence.

Spiritual: The soul's evolution through lessons learned along the path of life. To be spiritual is to be your true essence and allow your goodness and greatness to be all that they are within you, connected to the Source of your being, universal Essence.

Unconditional Love: To love all parts of the whole, releasing all conditions and attachments to any fragment that makes up the whole; based on acceptance and truth in the present moment.

Unfoldment: A Divine rightness of evolvement; through patience, trust, and stillness, you experience an all-knowing, inner reality that gently guides you on your path.

Universality: Embracing the quality of equality, openness, freedom, and the core of oneness; to be receptive to the realm of all natures of being.

Veil: A tool of the ego created by the mental body to cloud the reality of what truly is and keep the self from furthering its full concept of self; used to distract the expansion of consciousness by masquerading as reality, though it is an illusion.

Wholeness: The synthesis and integration of the mental, emotional, and physical bodies into a balanced, unified, and healthy personality. In this recognized state, the soul (higher self) can fuse with the balanced personality (lower self). Thus, the Essence of all can guide the whole, synthesized person.

Will of the Soul: The aspect of the higher self directed by the will/power principle of universal Truth. (See *higher self* and *intuition*.)

GUIDED MEDITATION

A Modified Version
A complement to *View from the Mountaintop:
A Journey to Self-Renewal*

This is your time to relax. Know that your only point of power is in the present moment. This is the moment for you to allow yourself to let go and simply be. Just be. Give yourself permission to unlearn all the thoughts you have learned. Free your mind. Let go of judgments. Situate yourself in a comfortable position. If you are in a chair, plant your feet firmly on the floor. If you are lying down, allow your arms and legs to be free from constriction. Get ready now for your personal journey into self-discovery and self-renewal.

As you close your eyes, focus your attention on your breath. Slowly inhale through your nose, and slowly exhale through your mouth. Breathe in peace, fulfillment, and confidence. Breathe out any sense of anxiety, tension, and limiting thought. Feel the supporting environment gently accept your body as you gradually give into gravity. Begin to feel the peacefulness around you. **Relax. Release, and let go.**

Now scan your body from your head to your toes. Focus on the top of your head, and feel the relaxation flow through your entire being. Sense the massage effect of relaxation moving through your scalp. Allow your face to go limp; release your jaw. A comfortable heaviness settles in your neck, radiating into the shoulders. Feel the warmth of relaxation penetrate down your arms and into your fingers and thumbs. As the wave of relaxation lingers, it begins to travel from the top of your spine to your hips. Your pelvis sinks deeper into the supporting environment as the flow of relaxation moves down your thighs and into your knees, releasing the lower legs and sending the relaxation out the bottom of your feet.

Be immersed in gentle relaxation. Allow yourself to be consumed by the soothing effect of muscular release. If you detect residual tension, focus on it; visualize, feel, and sense the warmth radiating into that area. The relaxation blends in harmony with the rest of the body. The total sum of the parts becomes one—one whole mind, body and spirit, relaxed and receptive to your inner love, beauty, truth, and goodness.

Visualize yourself at the base of a beautiful, majestic mountain. As you are relaxed on your path of life with the spiritual mountain behind you, you see or recognize it is reflected in the Lake of Peace before you. A portion of the lake is surrounded by a lush green forest. There is a canopy of light blue sky above, offering you protection and clarity on your journey. The golden essence radiant sun bathes you in its' luminosity paving the way before you, while guiding you to lovingly burn away the dross of old, let go what no longer serves a purpose in your life. **Be one with all the elements of nature. Breathe deep the fresh mountain air; allow it to purify you. Feel a sense of safety and security where you are.** Feel confident and competent in this moment. Own this place within you as a source of strength and encouragement. View the heavens above and feel the earth below, joyfully anticipating your journey. **Between the heights and the depths, between the within and the without, you are becoming balanced and centered, aligned and harmonic. You are one with the Nature of All Things.**

Now, as you focus in your heart center, see and feel your radiant point of light. See and feel a line of light reaching down to the heart of the earth, and a line of radiant light reaching up to the heart of heaven, with lines of light reaching out right and left to all of humanity, sharing your essence in the world. Poised in presence at your heart center, see and feel the equal-armed cross you are, connected above, below, within and without. It represents fairness, justice, equality, balance, harmony, and right relationship in all things. Be here and embody this truth. Lovingly invoke your expression and impression of Source, God, the Universe, whatever that may be for you, now. Say to yourself, "I lovingly invoke Divine Creative Expression, the Divine Mother – the Masters of Wisdom, the Great Ones that go before me, that I walk with and work with each and every day. I set forth my intention for this journey _____ that it be what it is to be, all in accordance with the will of my soul. I give thanks for this shared consciousness and for All that Is and so it is, and help me to do my part. Amen. Amin. Hum. Om. Shanti. Aho. Yes." (This passage is excerpted from Lee Ann's *Lotus Heart Sound Journey – Syinthesis® Method Manual* and upcoming book).

Step back, and examine the mountain. Gaze at the mountain's top, and observe the pathway below, carved by footprints in eight steps, representing your journey to self-renewal. The lengthy climb between each step provides opportunity to experience your Essence. Now venture toward the path leading up the base of the mountain.

Take your **first step to release**. Release from your life what no longer serves a purpose.

Let go of self-imposed limitations that have been holding you back from your true potential. Begin now by accepting your goodness and releasing the doubts and fears of the past. **Say to yourself, "I now willingly embrace and love life."**

Your **second step is to affirm and appreciate.** Affirm your goodness, and appreciate yourself for who and what you are in this present moment. Love yourself unconditionally for all the goodness you bring to the world. Your uniqueness is a gift. Appreciate and cherish it. You are a good person. **Say to yourself, "*I appreciate myself and affirm all the goodness in my life.*"**

The climb is steep to the **third step of clarity, purpose, and clear intention.** Create the vision of your dreams. Be clear. Clarity aligns your physical, mental, emotional, and spiritual selves. When you ask for clarity, get silent, and go within. **Say to yourself, "*I seek and find clarity and purpose in my life.*"**

Striving toward the mountain's summit, step up to the **fourth step to achieve balance.** All change can bring balance and peace in your life when viewed in clear thought. How you respond to the world around you creates your inner balance. It is the midpoint of opposites. It is achieving neutrality; it is moderation. **Say to yourself, "*I am living a life in balance and stability.*"**

You're feeling very strong now as you step up to the **fifth step of lightheartedness.** Simply let go of the boundaries, explore the unknown, learn to laugh, and really feel it. When you laugh, you free your heart of any heaviness; feel it getting lighter. Give yourself permission to free your inhibitions, get silly, and let your inner child out to play.

Say to yourself, "*I am filled with the loving energy of lightheartedness today.*"

As you venture forward, feel your entire mind, body, and spirit pull you up to the **sixth step of love.** Love is the foundation of life; it is the wisdom of the heart. Your love sustains and heals you. **Say to yourself, "*I am filled with the Essence of love. The more love I send out, the more love I receive, as it is all One. I love myself free from conditions.*"**

Feel your essence emerging as you lift yourself up to the **seventh step—receive.** Receive all the gifts and blessings that are yours. Listen in your heart and Spirit; know you are worthy to receive. Open yourself to receive your abundance now. **Say to yourself, "I willingly receive all the goodness that is mine, for it is my birthright."**

You meet your **eighth and final step** on your journey— **the step to thankfulness**. To perpetuate your goodness, always be grateful for the changes in your life. Give thanks to your higher power for the abundance that is yours. **Say to yourself, "I am thankful to my higher power, Source of being, for the abundance that is mine."**

As you rise to the summit of the mountain, you are filled with elation, self-acceptance, and self-respect. **Feel the beauty surrounding you and within you.** Embrace the partnership of your mind, body, and spirit—the oneness, the wholeness, the ability to flow freely within yourself. You are your Essence.

Recognize your inner strength and beauty. You are filled with courage, wisdom, truth, and inner peace. **Feel lighter, freer, unencumbered.** This sense of lightness lifts you above the endless ebb and flow of life. You now acquire a broader vision; you see the goodness in everyone. You develop clear intention, purpose, and manifest goals. Your knowingness is magnified. **Feel the sense of self-renewal.** This is yours.

You feel accomplished, confident, and competent. Your heart is affirmed by your goodness. Your heart is knowing. Your heart is filled with laughter. Your heart is willing to give and receive. Just sit back, and view your journey with a sense of awe and appreciation. Keep your feet firm in the earth as your mind, heart, and spirit remain in the heavens. Stretch yourself. **Believe in yourself.** Hold on to your truth.

Continue to fill yourself with the riches of Essence and Grace. **Be filled with all that empowers your mind, body, and spirit** as you review the eight steps:

1 – Release/Let Go/Empty
2 – Affirm and Appreciate
3 – Discover Purpose and Clear Intention
4 – Begin to Achieve Balance
5 – Embrace Lightheartedness
6 – Love
7 – Receive
8 – Give Thanks/Gratitude

Feel a sense of invigoration and self-renewal, and know each and every day you are getting better and better.

Now bring your awareness and your consciousness back into this space and place. Take your time, and breathe a deep, complete inhalation. Feel the revitalization and invigoration, and slowly exhale. Inhale deeply and completely, and stretch your arms up overhead, as if it's your first big yawn of the day. Slowly and completely exhale.

As a flower closes its petals at dusk, imagine you are also bringing your energies close to your body. Imagine you are putting on a cloak of many colors or a simple pure white cloak. Zip it up the front of your body, and place your loose hood up over your head and eyebrows to symbolically close the energy pathways in the front and back of your body to make your biofield or electromagnetic field of energy a bit smaller. This will help you be more comfortable when you get up and proceed into your day.

Know you can take yourself to the mountain's summit at any time during your day and experience your journey of self-renewal. Simply close your eyes, and visualize yourself on your mountaintop. You are at peace with yourself and all around you, and in silence, you say to yourself, "I am the light of my truth. I am ..."

As you become familiar with the meditation, let yourself relax, and simply focus on the words in bold print to guide you. The italicized words are important to embody and become familiar with. As you practice, you may eventually find you only need to glance at some of the bold and italicized words as well as the list of steps. Use whatever works for you to journey into this relaxation, meditation, and contemplation time.

DAILY DECLARATIONS OF EMPOWERMENT CUTOUT CARDS

On the following pages are daily declarations of empowerment cutout cards. The daily declarations of empowerment accompany each poem, serving as points of focus, vibrational keynotes of poetic verse. The cards are sequentially presented, as are the poems in the book.

You may cut out your cards and personalize them with colors—bold hues, watercolors, markers, pencil—whatever makes your heart sing. Perhaps laminate them, or simply creatively express with them, and know your soul is gently guiding you to be filled.

On one side of the cards is the gateway. The gateways are sections of the book and stages of awareness. You may seek guidance with a particular situation. In that case, you may know which of the three gateway stages you are in and choose to shuffle and use one gateway at a time.

However, you may use the deck as a whole, an oracle (a divination tool), understanding the gateways are passages but also circular in nature. The vibrational intent is not linear; rather, it is to ignite our remembrance of our non-dual nature.

Bless your cards by placing them between your hands. You may read one of the special invocations or one of the verses in the front of the book as a blessing for your cards.

Gently and mindfully shuffle your deck as you ask for guidance; then select the declaration that directs you to the poem and the harmonization of its verse.

You will receive the divine energetic resonance encoded in the verse, woven within the sacred sound stream to enlighten your true self.

Recite the daily declarations silently or aloud as seeds of truth that are vibrationally connected to the poetic verse.

The daily declaration will set the tone of intention to elicit deeper awakening and expansion into the full expression of all that you are. Our individual self-transformation yields global transformation.

It is by way of the Divine feminine that our humanity will come into balance—peace, love, goodwill, and solidarity. As many of us are weavers of synthesis, we shall harmonize the self and the collective, assisting humanity in its healing process. Between the heights and the depths, between the within and the without, we are becoming balanced and centered, aligned and harmonic, one with the One life.

We are the interconnectedness of life. Yes!

You may also purchase a printable PDF of the cut-out cards or a set of full-color pre-made laminated cards at Syinthesis.com.

GATEWAY 1

Decondition the Self

SELF-AWARENESS

GATEWAY 1

Decondition the Self

SELF-AWARENESS

GATEWAY 1

Decondition the Self

SELF-AWARENESS

GATEWAY 1

Decondition the Self

SELF-AWARENESS

Lessons

In the light of my soul, I declare...

I open to receive
my life lessons
and accept the gift
in their revealing.

Time to Fly

In the light of my soul, I declare...

I trust
in all that I am,
in all that I Am.

Echo of Love

In the light of my soul, I declare...

I am flowing
in the stream
of divine love.
I share this positive
ripple effect
with all those
in its wake.

Acceptance

In the light of my soul, I declare...

I love and
accept myself
unconditionally,
as I open my
heart to my
truth of being.

GATEWAY 1

Decondition the Self

SELF-AWARENESS

GATEWAY 1

Decondition the Self

SELF-AWARENESS

GATEWAY 1

Decondition the Self

SELF-AWARENESS

GATEWAY 1

Decondition the Self

SELF-AWARENESS

Be Still

In the light of my soul, I declare...

I am radiantly
alive in the stillness
of my quiet center.
I am pure
spaciousness.

Letting Go

In the light of my soul, I declare...

I practice
self-emptying.
I let go of
inner gripping
(attachments).
I create space for
love in my life now.

Conditioned Thoughts

In the light of my soul, I declare...

I allow my rigid
held beliefs to melt
into a clarity
of what is to be.
I am creating
opportunity
for the new.

Detachment

In the light of my soul, I declare...

I am mindfully
detaching from
what was that I
may open my heart
upon the middle way
of nonattachment.

GATEWAY 1

Decondition the Self

SELF-AWARENESS

GATEWAY 1

Decondition the Self

SELF-AWARENESS

GATEWAY 1

Decondition the Self

SELF-AWARENESS

GATEWAY 1

Decondition the Self

SELF-AWARENESS

The Self

In the light of my soul, I declare...

I am more than a
part of parts to see.
I am whole
within the Whole,
sharing the full
expression of me.

Synchronicity

In the light of my soul, I declare...

I trust
in the unfolding
synchronicity of
life lessons, as they
are based in the
universal wisdom
of Divine right
time and order.

Purpose

In the light of my soul, I declare...

I listen
with inner ears.
I see with inner eyes.
My life lessons teach
soul's purpose, no
matter the disguise.

Mirror Reflection

In the light of my soul, I declare...

I am choosing to see
in you the real me.
This is how I awaken
myself to release,
to expand, to be free.

Recondition the Self

SELF-EXPANSION

GATEWAY 2

Recondition the Self

SELF-EXPANSION

GATEWAY 2

Recondition the Self

SELF-EXPANSION

GATEWAY 2

Recondition the Self

SELF-EXPANSION

Objective Reality

In the light of my soul, I declare...

I am balanced
and harmonic with a
free-spirited vision.
I embrace the reality
that life is
unlimited possibility.

Reality or Illusion?

In the light of my soul, I declare...

I sit at the midpoint
of opposites, an
uplifted, neutral space.
Whether reality
or illusion,
I live a life of love
and empowered Grace.

The Simple

In the light of my soul, I declare...

Today
I keep it simple.
I act without acting,
as the way to do
is to be.

Truth

In the light of my soul, I declare...

The truth is hidden
in my soul, as
I have come to know
that life's journey
is not a goal
but my unfolding
self to grow.

Recondition the Self

SELF-EXPANSION

Recondition the Self

SELF-EXPANSION

Recondition the Self

SELF-EXPANSION

Recondition the Self

SELF-EXPANSION

Listen

In the light of my soul, I declare...

I listen and feel
truth in my heart;
this gift of revealing
is mine. Angelic
Dominion expresses;
inner doorways open
in time. I listen.
I trust. I act. I am.

Light

In the light of my soul, I declare...

I am the light
of Truth; it is
the way of the Way.
It is the love of being,
acknowledged
each new day.

Forgiveness

In the light of my soul, I declare...

I forgive myself
and others now,
for it is of the past.
As I forgive,
I free myself to live.

Clarity

In the light of my soul, I declare...

I clarify my purpose
now, digging deep
from the inside.
I live a life of
surrender and love
by which I truly abide.

Recondition the Self

SELF-EXPANSION

GATEWAY 2

Recondition the Self

SELF-EXPANSION

GATEWAY 2

Recondition the Self

SELF-EXPANSION

GATEWAY 2

Recondition the Self

SELF-EXPANSION

Surrender

In the light of my soul, I declare…

I surrender
and forgive;
I detach
and rise above.
I embrace freedom
in the truth of
unconditional love.

Angel Wings

In the light of my soul, I declare…

I feel the wings
of my angel gently
guiding me this day,
as I learn to be
accepting, knowing
the answer is in Way.

Inner Guidance

In the light of my soul, I declare…

I am one with
my inner guidance,
silent and
focused within.
I trust my confident
steadiness, reframing
any chaotic spin.

Lighthearted

In the light of my soul, I declare…

I willingly
free myself
of limited living,
expanding
lightheartedly
how I may.

GATEWAY 2
Recondition the Self

SELF-EXPANSION

GATEWAY 2
Recondition the Self

SELF-EXPANSION

GATEWAY 2
Recondition the Self

SELF-EXPANSION

GATEWAY 2
Recondition the Self

SELF-EXPANSION

Be and Receive

In the light of my soul, I declare...

I embrace
the gift of receiving
with an open heart
this day.
My soul
spreads its wings,
expanding
every which way.

Inner Life

In the light of my soul, I declare...

The rhythm
of my inner life
flourishes beyond
time and space.
I release rigid
concepts, embodying
empowered Grace.

It Is What It Is

In the light of my soul, I declare...

I realize life lessons
reveal for me to see,
that it is what it is,
as it is to be.

Balance

In the light of my soul, I declare...

I recognize the
midpoint of balance
is a search in the
to and the fro,
engaging in life's
mystical dance,
embracing what my
spirit truly knows.

GATEWAY 2
Recondition the Self

SELF-EXPANSION

GATEWAY 3
The Unconditioned Self

THE SELF REALIZED

GATEWAY 3
The Unconditioned Self

THE SELF REALIZED

GATEWAY 3
The Unconditioned Self

THE SELF REALIZED

Transformation

I am transforming
my mental and
emotional self,
my physical being too.
I own all that I am,
as I lovingly
release to renew.

Honor

I am deserving
of all the love
emanating in my soul.
I accept, respect,
and honor this
as my birthright,
not a goal.

Awareness Rising

Conscious awareness
is rising as my level
of spirituality shines.
I share my essence
with others, to renew
hope in the sacred
human design.

To Be

I abide at the
center of my being
as I search my
heart to see.
Through the
inner gateway,
I enter
the way to do is to be.

GATEWAY 3

The Unconditioned Self

THE SELF REALIZED

GATEWAY 3

The Unconditioned Self

THE SELF REALIZED

GATEWAY 3

The Unconditioned Self

THE SELF REALIZED

GATEWAY 3

The Unconditioned Self

THE SELF REALIZED

I Miss You

In the light of my soul, I declare...

I anchor into the
Truth of Spirit,
unconsciously
relaxing my breath.
I fear not the
transition of life,
the unfolding
process of death.

Unfoldment

In the light of my soul, I declare...

Unfoldment
is the gentle whisper
of infinite God,
loving and true.
It is the silent
knowingness as
I trust how to
act and what to do.

Suspend Yourself and Relax

In the light of my soul, I declare...

I imagine I am one
with the melodious
rhythm of nature
lulling me
far and beyond.
I am grounded in the
flow of communion,
generating inner joy
oh so profound.

Compassionate Detachment

In the light of my soul, I declare...

I willingly
embrace unfoldment.
I see truth
in the eyes of Grace;
it is compassionate
detachment healing
and renewing
my inner space.

GATEWAY 3

The Unconditioned Self

THE SELF REALIZED

GATEWAY 3

The Unconditioned Self

THE SELF REALIZED

GATEWAY 3

The Unconditioned Self

THE SELF REALIZED

GATEWAY 3

The Unconditioned Self

THE SELF REALIZED

I Am

In the light of my soul, I declare...

I Am all that I Am.
I Am the light of Truth.
I am one with
the Essence of all,
a life of love
I live as pure proof.
I Am.

Communion With Thee

In the light of my soul, I declare...

I am intuitively guided
to start fresh today.
The cause is
for me to see
that I am in
communion with Thee.

Feel the Flow of Spirit

In the light of my soul, I declare...

As I release any
ego thought that there
is only one way to see,
I realize the
alchemy of awareness
is for me to truly be.
I flow with Spirit.

The Essence of Spirit

In the light of my soul, I declare...

I breathe deep
the Essence of Spirit,
the sound of silence—
radiant, boundless
and whole.

GATEWAY 3

The Unconditioned Self

THE SELF REALIZED

GATEWAY 3

The Unconditioned Self

THE SELF REALIZED

GATEWAY 3

The Unconditioned Self

THE SELF REALIZED

GATEWAY 3

The Unconditioned Self

THE SELF REALIZED

The Moon

In the light of my soul, I declare...

I drift far away,
bathing in her rays.
I embody her vibration.
I ground the change.
I release. I manifest.
I co-create. I Am.

Pure Love

In the light of my soul, I declare...

Love is the supreme
flow of energy
unencumbered in
motion and bliss.
It has no limits because
it is the great Source
of pure being-ness.
I am love,
and I am loved.

The Nature of God

In the light of my soul, I declare...

I listen to love's echo
resonate deep within
nature's walls, lauded
in all its holiness,
the essence of
Mother/Father
God's call.

Believe Me When I Say I Am

In the light of my soul, I declare...

Believe me when
I say I am living
in my angels' glow,
flowing in the
wisdom stream,
harmonizing with
all I truly know.

ABOUT THE AUTHOR

Lee Ann Fagan Dzelzkalns

Lee Ann is a vibration healer, sound healing practitioner, and teacher specializing in facilitating guided meditation. Her heart-centered and soul-directed approach has led many along the path to deep healing, soul growth, and self-realization. Her guiding axiom is, "Self-transformation yields global transformation."

After completing a Bachelor of Social Work and practicing medical social work in Grand Rapids, Michigan, Lee Ann acquired a Master of Science in Exercise Sports Science at the University of Utah. Active in the fitness industry, she was a regular contributor to *Shape* magazine in 1980s and mid-1990s and a lecturer in mind-body integration at the University of Wisconsin-Milwaukee for twenty-three years. Following her passion for the spiritual, she was ordained as an interfaith minister by the New Seminary in New York City, and since 1999, she has been a spiritual guide and officiant, creating and conducting sacred wedding ceremonies, celebration of life services, baby blessings, and baptisms and assisting in the death and dying process.

Lee Ann is the founder of L A Consulting, Inc. and the Syinthesis® Sound Healing Center, where she offers sound soul journeys, workshops, treasure mapping, nature walks, guided meditations, and experiential exercises to elicit healing, defuse stressors, dissolve emotional attachments, invite deepening insights, and encourage self-transformation. She is the creator of the Syinthesis® Sound Healing Method, a transformative and effective sound journey formula that fosters internal adjustments and restores the energy body to its natural frequency and balance while encouraging spiritual awakening in participants.

Lee Ann has published and produced many guided meditative recordings and writings to encourage personal growth and spiritual development. She is currently writing *The Lotus Heart Sound Journey: A Guide in Sound Healing Facilitation*, which is based on the Syinthesis® Method.

For more information, please visit her website at *www.syinthesis.com*.